THE
MAGNETIC
ADVANTAGE

How Great Companies **Attract**, **Retain**, & **Engage** the Best People

Pascha Moore Kelley

Foreword by Tom Ziglar
Son of Zig Ziglar and CEO of Ziglar, Inc.

Courtesy of Pexels.com - rock background (page 23)
Courtesy of Vecteezy.com - sandwich graphic (page 121)

ISBN: 978-1-946629-26-5 (print)

DEDICATION

To my husband, Mike Kelley, who has supported me on my journey from the corporate world to living my God-given purpose as a speaker and writer.

Thank you for believing in me!

IN LOVING MEMORY OF DR. JEAN A. KELLEY

1930 - 2018

I'M PROUD TO CALL THIS inspirational woman my mother-in-law. Jean was the granddaughter of immigrants from Eastern Europe, whose family primarily worked in the toxic coal mines and factories in the Northeast. She suffered her first tragedy at two years old when her father was burned to death in a house fire. Her mother remarried two more times to good men, but both father figures died of health problems. Probably the most heartbreaking tragedy for Jean was the death of her nine-year old sister of leukemia.

Jean used the tragedy of her youth to propel her into a career in healthcare where she made significant contributions. After serving as a nurse in the Korean War, she obtained several degrees including her doctorate. Jean joined the faculty at the University of Alabama at Birmingham School of Nursing (UABSON) where she committed her entire career to the growth and development of nursing leaders. Jean spent the last 19 years at UABSON as Associate Dean for Graduate Programs. Even in her 80's, she was still contributing to her beloved University as a consultant.

Jean is known as a pioneer in the advancement of graduate nursing education. She helped found UABSONs first doctoral nursing program, which was also the first in the Southeast and one of twelve nationwide. She was inducted in the Alabama Healthcare Hall of Fame and has received numerous other awards for her work. Personally, I think one of her greatest rewards was the tremendous love and friendship that she shared with her former students and colleagues. Jean has left a rich legacy in both healthcare and in the lives of the people who knew her. She truly embodied the qualities of a Magnetic Leader.

ACKNOWLEDGEMENT

I MUST FIRST AND FOREMOST give the credit for this book to God. As someone who could barely write a thank-you note years ago, I would have never thought that I could be an author. I'm an analytical-numbers person after all. However, when God calls us to do something, He provides everything we need to do it. That is certainly the case for me in writing this book.

I want to thank my parents, Lex and Janet Moore, for giving me a strong work ethic, Christian values, and a moral base. Also, for paying for my college education. Now that I have kids in college, I have a whole new appreciation for what you gave me. College was a lot more fun when you were paying the bills! I appreciate your love and support through all of the stages of my life. I'm sure that you frequently wondered, "What is she up to now?" And you loved me anyway.

I want to recognize my children Madeline and Jacob, who were such a part of my corporate journey, and who did not have a "normal" mom growing up. While I desperately wanted to be a stay-at-home mom, I was simply horrible at it. Now, I can see that God had a purpose in how He made me. A lack of domestic skills was not simply an oversight on His part. You both are uniquely made, and I pray that you will find the joy of fulfilling God's purpose for your lives. Maddie and Jacob, you haven't always had it easy, and I'm so proud of the young adults that you are becoming!

Thank you to Martha Donze, who was my manager for almost 17 years. You taught me most of what I know about HR, and a lot about life. You also taught—no, demanded—that I learn how to write. Through much red ink and your persistence over many years, I actually got pretty good at writing. I couldn't have written this book without you!

FOREWORD

AS A BOY, I WAS fascinated with magnets. I had several toys that used magnets and metal shapes to build interesting designs. I learned that you could get several small magnets together and their power would really add up. A few times, I played with larger magnets that were used for commercial purposes - and you really had to be careful with them!

In the business world, I learned that individuals and companies can be magnetic as well. Of course, a magnetic company is only that way because of its people. Here is the reality. Magnetic companies happen by design. A magnetic leader gets a vision and then designs a plan that will create a world-class organization - which always revolves around its people and the culture.

Pascha Kelley is a magnetic leader who has the gift of inspiring and equipping magnetic leaders to develop themselves and their organizations to their full potential. As you read The Magnetic Advantage, you will understand why we are so proud at Ziglar to have Pascha as one of our Ziglar Legacy Certified speakers and trainers. Get your pen and action planner out as you read, because creating the magnetic company you want is only a few pages away!

—Tom Ziglar
Proud Son of Zig Ziglar and CEO of Ziglar, Inc.

TABLE OF CONTENTS

INTRODUCTION 1

MAGNETIC LEADERSHIP. 7

Chapter 1: The Cornerstone. 9

Chapter 2: The Power of Employee Engagement 13

Chapter 3: Cost of Employee Turnover. 17

Chapter 4: Characteristics of a Magnetic Leader 23

Chapter 5: How to Become a Magnetic Leader 27

MAGNETIC CULTURE 37

Chapter 6: Culture Defined 39

Chapter 7: How to Create a Magnetic Culture 45

Chapter 8: Integration into Fabric of the Company 53

Chapter 9: Hiring Process 57

Chapter 10: Performance Management 65

Chapter 11: Compensation and Recognition Programs 69

Chapter 12: Cultural Symbols 73

Chapter 13: Social Events 77

MAGNETIC EMPLOYEE PROGRAMS. 81

Chapter 14: Maximize Your Return on Investment (ROI) 83

Chapter 15: Total Rewards Strategy 85

Chapter 16: How to Build a Total Rewards Strategy. 89

Chapter 17: Compensation 97

Chapter 18: Benefits 105

Chapter 19: Work-Life Programs 109

Chapter 20: Recognition Programs 113

Chapter 21: Performance Management 119

Chapter 22: Talent Development 125

Chapter 23: Total Rewards Communication 133

CONCLUSION. 141

BIOGRAPHY. 143

BIBLIOGRAPHY 145

INTRODUCTION

I HAVE A PASSION FOR helping businesses succeed, because when businesses succeed, people succeed. I love seeing a business owner's hard work, risk, and dedication pay off in a big way. I grew up in an entrepreneurial family and worked in a start-up company. My husband owns a commercial real estate appraisal company, and we have self-storage businesses as well. Now, I'm a Ziglar Legacy Certified Trainer, and Ziglar is all about helping people succeed in their professional and personal lives.

I am also passionate about making the workplace better, so that employees can find fulfillment in their work, develop friendships, and have fun! Most people spend more waking hours working than doing anything else. Shouldn't they enjoy it? Honestly, I simply love to work—and I don't have domestic skills (gasp!), so I'd rather be in my office than in the kitchen. My office is full of family pictures, and my dog and cat are my constant companions. This is bliss for me! While I work from home now, I'm not alone because I'm part of the Ziglar community.

The purpose of this book is to share with you strategies and tactics that I've seen work in business. These strategies are low on financial costs and high on financial gain. However, there is cost in time to plan and implement these strategies. Most of all, it takes *commitment, integrity, and the ability to truly understand that people are a business's greatest asset.*

So, here is my story.

SMALL-TOWN GIRL

I grew up in an entrepreneurial family in Hamilton, Alabama, a town of approximately 5,000 people. My family owned a clothing manufacturing company, Toll-Gate Garment Company, that my grandfather, Lemuel Moore, built in the 1950s. I grew up hearing the stories of struggle and sacrifice that it took to build that company. In a way similar to Zig Ziglar, my grandfather grew up during the Great Depression in Mississippi, so he started from nothing and built a thriving business.

My dad, Lex Moore, started working at five years old, cleaning offices and restrooms in the company at night, and he grew up doing all kinds of jobs in the company. My grandfather eventually turned the company over to my dad and uncle, Bob Moore.

Growing up, I saw that company's successes and setbacks, and the emotions that went with it. For the most part, while I was growing up Toll-Gate thrived. After NAFTA was passed, the company simply could not compete with foreign labor. Like many other manufacturing companies in the U.S., our company had to close its doors.

I was in my twenties and had my own career by the time Toll-Gate closed. But, the closing of the family business hit me hard, and I think it is one reason why I feel so passionate about helping business owners succeed. I know that behind businesses, there are people and families who rely upon those companies to survive.

The closing of the family business also taught me that no business or job is guaranteed. Things can change in an instant with one stroke of a government pen. So, I learned to have multiple streams of income. Fortunately, I inherited my grandfather's entrepreneurial spirit and love for investing.

It was my dad who taught me how to be a good leader and manager of people. I've seen him manage Toll-Gate during the day and another family business at night because a manager suddenly left. I've also witnessed him talking to clients in New York one minute and working under a broken machine the next. This taught me that being a business owner doesn't mean sitting in a plush office reaping the rewards. It means that you've got to roll up your sleeves and make sure the work gets done.

My dad also demonstrated a genuine care for his employees and their families. His employees seemed to adore him, and the company had a high retention rate. My dad is the person who introduced me to employee recognition—in words and gifts. I think that it just came naturally to him.

My family was also very involved in church and the community, so I learned from this the importance of working hard in more than just business. It is important to give back to the community and to serve in church. In fact, both of my brothers, Tracy and Slate Moore, are preachers. My family gave me a good spiritual base and values that serve as a strong foundation for my life.

For the most part, I grew up as a small-town princess enjoying the benefits of my family's hard work. (My husband thinks that I've still got a bit too much of the "princess" left in me.) I went to the University of Alabama and majored in finance. When I graduated, I moved to Birmingham, Alabama, to pursue my career.

THE START-UP COMPANY

After a few years of finding out what I was *not* good at, I landed at Scandipharm, Inc.,[1] a start-up pharmaceutical company. While I had reaped the benefits of my family's businesses, it was now time for me to

---

1. When I refer to "Scandipharm," it encompasses later name changes to "Axcan Scandipharm, Inc.", "Axcan Pharma, Inc.," and "Aptalis, Inc." These companies maintained the original core values and other elements of the original company. However, when the company was purchased in 2014 by Forest Laboratories, Inc., who was then purchased by Actavis Pharmaceuticals a few weeks later, the company became part of a much larger organization, and Scandipharm was absorbed into that company's culture.

roll up my sleeves and go to work. The founder of Scandipharm, Charlie Wingett, was an amazing visionary who believed in the Jim Collins method of building a company. He used Jim Collins' book *Built to Last* to build the company's rich culture.

While Scandipharm wasn't my personal company, I had the heart of an entrepreneur and wanted to see this company succeed. What I found was that as the company grew, so did I – in knowledge and wisdom.

The corporate culture was truly the secret sauce that made this company successful. I worked in Human Resources and saw people come to work there for less money than they could make with a big pharma company. Why? Because of the culture. People stayed and were motivated by the rich culture that existed at Scandipharm. Even as the company grew, was sold, merged, upsized, and downsized, remnants of the original culture remained.

While Scandipharm's culture was the glue, there were many other tools used to fight our way out of the pit in the pharmaceutical world. We were up against companies with much deeper pockets and greater resources. To play with the big guys, we had to be creative, resourceful, and determined. Because we were small, one advantage we had was being wiry and able to change directions quickly, so this was a fast-moving and constantly changing company. It was the perfect place for me to thrive! I loved the change, the pace, and the challenge.

After a total of twenty years with the company, the Birmingham office was closed due to an acquisition, and I lost my job. However, I knew at that time that God was preparing me for something much greater. After three years of working with my husband in our family businesses, I had the opportunity to become a Ziglar Legacy Certified Trainer. This was my dream, and I knew this job was what God had been preparing me for.

MY DREAM JOB

I'm not sure when I started learning from Zig Ziglar. It seems like I've always known of him and his messages. I've listened to the Ziglar podcast, one of the top-rated business podcasts, for years. Zig's messages really resonate with me. Zig died in 2012, but his family and company are determined to share his messages of hope and encouragement with even more people. *Let's face it, the world needs these messages now more than ever.*

I'm so excited that I get to be part of Zig Ziglar's legacy and continue to learn from the Ziglar community. This gives me even more business training and communication skills. Also, through the Ziglar company, I'm exposed to amazing thought leaders and learning materials on a continuous basis.

Combining Ziglar principles with my corporate experience and research, I created a powerful formula for attracting, retaining and engaging people: **The Magnetic Advantage**. At the heart of this formula is the Ziglar principle, "You don't build a business – you build people – and people build the business."

The Magnetic Advantage formula consists of three primary components: Leadership, Culture and Employee Programs. This book is divided into the following three sections to explain each part of the formula:

I. **Magnetic Leadership - Develop the qualities of a Magnetic Leader.** This section explains why employee engagement is so important to a company's long-term success. I've provided studies that reveal the positive impact of having a highly-engaged workforce, and the costs of low engagement. Then, I'll explain the leadership skills required to create and maintain engagement in your company.

II. **Magnetic Culture - Build the foundation of a great culture and bring it to life.** In this section, you'll learn how to create a culture that will attract, engage, and retain the right people for your company. I'll explain how to build the foundation for that culture and how to integrate your guiding principles (Vision, Mission, and Core Values) throughout your company.

III. **Magnetic Employee Programs - Create and implement a powerful rewards strategy.** This section will teach you how to improve your return on investment in employee programs through a strategy called Total Rewards. You will learn how to build a Total Rewards strategy as well as a robust employee communication program.

The principles that I lay out in this book are designed to save you money and enhance your workforce. As Jack Welch says, "The team with the best players wins." Let's get started creating your winning team!

MAGNETIC LEADERSHIP

Develop the Qualities of a Magnetic Leader

CHAPTER 1

The Cornerstone

GREAT LEADERSHIP IS THE CORNERSTONE of The Magnetic Advantage formula. As John Maxwell says, *"Everything rises and falls on leadership."* *(Maxwell, 2007)* A company can't have a great culture without authentic leadership. This is what determines the strength of the magnetic pull for new employees, and a company's ability to keep good people.

Magnetic Leaders truly embrace Zig Ziglar's principle: You don't build a business – you build people – and people build the business. Truett Cathy, founder of Chick-Fil-A, is an excellent example of a Magnetic Leader. In fact, he said,

> "We are not in the chicken business.
> We are in the people business."
> – TRUETT CATHY (TURNER, 2015)

Truett Cathy recognized the value of putting people first. His policy of closing Chick-Fil-A stores on Sundays is an example of this. Truett believed that everyone needs a day off to rest, to pursue their interests, and spend time with their families. By closing the stores on

Sundays, he ensured that all of his employees would have a *consistent* day off each week. For people working different shifts and ever-changing schedules, having that consistency is priceless! What a gift to his restaurant employees.

During the early stages of Chick-fil-A's growth, Truett received a lot of pressure to do away with his closed-on-Sunday policy. In fact, Chick-fil-A was rejected by several malls. I'm sure that a lot of people told him how much more money he could make if he would open on Sundays. However, Truett remained true to his values – and to his people. Pretty soon, it became known to mall managers that Chick-Fil-A produced as much sales revenue in six days as the other food chains did in seven days. *In fact, Chick-Fil-A frequently had the highest volume sales of all the tenants in the food court!* (Turner, 2015)

In Dee Ann Turner's book, *It's My Pleasure — The Impact of Extraordinary Talent and a Compelling Culture*, she says "Truett was often asked if he had calculated how much sales he lost by being closed on Sunday. He always responded that he was more concerned with how much sales he would have lost had he remained open." Despite being closed on Sundays, Chick-fil-A is the top selling quick-service chain in the U.S. and exceeds their nearest competitor by *generating twice the average restaurant sales.* (Turner, 2015) **Truett Cathy created competitive advantage by putting the needs of his employees first. He stood strong in his values and reaped the rewards.**

People are truly the most important asset of a company, so learning strategies to enhance that asset is critical to creating competitive advantage. The strategies that I will provide in this book are not for those afraid of change or lacking in moral character. The workforce has changed drastically in the past several years, and companies who are not willing to adjust to the needs of this new workforce will be left behind. Additionally, due to the rapid development of technology, the workforce will continue to change quickly. Business leaders who can adjust quickly, while holding true to their values, will be able to create competitive advantage in this new landscape. The best employees will go to and remain with the companies that understand what their employees really want and that are willing to meet those needs.

WHAT PEOPLE REALLY WANT

For more than forty years, Ziglar, Inc. has researched what people really want in life. It found that there are eight things that everybody wants (Ziglar, 2012):

1. To be **happy**
2. To be **healthy**
3. To be **reasonably prosperous**
4. To be **secure**
5. To have **friends**
6. To have **peace of mind**
7. To have **good family relationships**
8. To have **hope**

You will notice that only one of these specifically lists money (reasonably prosperous). The others are non-financial. Business leaders frequently believe that employees are only interested in the financial rewards of work, but people's needs are much more complicated. Leaders who understand this seek to understand the true desires of their employees and meet those needs as best they can.

Zig Ziglar truly understood the importance of getting to know people and finding out what they really want. I think that Zig's philosophy, "You can have everything in life that you want if you will just help enough other people get what they want," (Ziglar Z. Z., 2012) is the heart and soul of good people management.

> **You can have everything in life that you want if you will just help enough other people get what they want.**
>
> – ZIG ZIGLAR

Helping employees get what they want will eventually lead to the business getting what it wants – long-term success.

CHAPTER 2

The Power of Employee Engagement

"EMPLOYEE ENGAGEMENT" HAS BECOME A buzz phrase in business over the past few years. However, most people don't really understand what engagement means. Forbes defines employee engagement as "the emotional commitment the employee has to the organization and goals." It is NOT employee satisfaction or happiness. Engagement is about a bone deep **commitment** to the company. Engaged employees are willing to go the extra mile. They have good attitudes and are willing to work as part of the team to accomplish goals.

According to Dale Carnegie Training, engaged employees have four traits:

1. **Enthusiasm** – Employees who are engaged are enthusiastic about work.

2. **Empowered** – Employees are allowed to do the work their way.

3. **Inspired** – Employees are motivated by their leaders.

4. **Confident** – Employees are sure they can achieve success.

Wouldn't you like to see these qualities in your employees? What would that mean for the bottom line of your company?

Companies with engaged employees outperform those without engaged employees by up to 202%.

– DALE CARNEGIE TRAINING

A study by Dale Carnegie Training found that companies with engaged employees outperform those without engaged employees by up to 202%.

In Gallup's 2016 State of the American Workplace survey, they found that businesses with an engagement strategy have better business outcomes. In fact, ***those that scored in the top quartile of employee engagement have nearly double the odds of success when compared to those at the bottom of the quartile***.

When compared with companies in the bottom quartile of engagement, companies in the top quartile showed improvements in the following areas:

- 41% lower absenteeism

- 24% lower turnover (high-turnover organizations)

- 59% lower turnover (low-turnover organizations)

- 28% less shrinkage

- 70% fewer safety incidents

- 58% lower patient safety incidents

- 40% fewer quality defects

- 10% higher customer metrics

- 17% higher productivity

- 20% higher sales

- 21% higher profitability

These findings show the significance of having an engaged workforce. *What if your business could experience even one of these factors (e.g., 20% higher sales) with an employee engagement strategy?*

Would you be willing to create and implement such a strategy?

Business leaders who truly understand the impact of engaging their workforce, and create and implement engagement strategies will be able to outpace the competition. You see, even though "Employee Engagement" is a buzz phrase, not all business leaders can accomplish this because they simply can't or won't acknowledge the importance of meeting the needs of their people. I believe this is due to self-centeredness, an unwillingness to really connect with people, and a lack of a moral compass.

Those leaders who are able to get the "people" thing right have a long-term advantage over those who do not. Doug Conant is an example of a leader who gets it. Doug has turned around several companies including Nabisco Foods Company, Campbell's Soup Company, and Avon Products. You see, Doug discovered the secret to advancing stakeholder value: employee engagement. Doug's motto is, "**To win in the marketplace, you must first win in the workplace**" (conantleadership.com). Doug says that achieving high employee engagement was the primary reason he was able to turn around these struggling companies.

We've discussed the upside of engagement. Now, we need to look at the implications of not having an engaged workforce. The Dale Carnegie Training study also revealed that 71% of employees are not fully engaged. Disengaged workers are typically less productive and tend to leave. In the next section, I will discuss the high cost of employee turnover.

CHAPTER 3

Cost of Employee Turnover

EMPLOYEE TURNOVER HAS A HIGH cost to the company, and that cost has risen significantly over the past several years. This is due to millennials being the largest segment of the workforce, and they generally only stay at a job for one year. Plus, as mentioned above, employees simply have more choices now as there is a low supply of and high demand for skilled workers.

The employee turnover rate is calculated by dividing the number of employees who have left the company by the total number of employees. For example, a company had 7 employees who left, and the total number of employees is 100. The turnover rate is 7% (7 ÷ 100). This rate is generally calculated on an annual basis using the total number of employees on January 1 divided by the total number who left the company during the entire year.

The higher the turnover rate, the higher the cost to the company. A study by Dale Carnegie Training estimates that *$11 billion is lost annually due to employee turnover.*

The cost of employee turnover includes the direct financial expenses, which are fairly easy to calculate, and the

$11 billion is lost annually due to employee turnover.

soft costs such as loss of productivity, time, and opportunity. Because of the difficulty of assigning a cost to some of these expenses and loss of revenue, it is challenging to determine the exact cost of employee turnover.

There are many theories on how turnover costs should be calculated, but there is not a standard way of calculating the cost of employee turnover. However, *all experts agree that the cost of employee turnover is high, even using the most conservative calculation methods.*

Turnover costs are generally calculated as a percent of salary. The percentages vary widely. In researching the topic, I've seen the costs reported as low as 33% of salary and as high as 400% of salary. The most commonly used measurements seem to range from 50% to 200% of salary. To give you an idea of the costs, I've provided an example below of the turnover costs for several different salaries at 50%, 100%, and 200% of salary.

SALARY	% OF SALARY		
	50%	100%	200%
$30,000	$15,000	$30,000	$60,000
$50,000	$25,000	$50,000	$100,000
$70,000	$35,000	$70,000	$140,000
$90,000	$45,000	$90,000	$180,000
$110,000	$55,000	$110,000	$220,000
$130,000	$65,000	$130,000	$260,000
$150,000	$75,000	$150,000	$300,000
$200,000	$100,000	$200,000	$400,000

Example of turnover costs at different salaries,
and percentage of salaries.

The reason turnover cost is so hard to pin down to a certain percentage of salary is because every job and employee are different. The actual cost of turnover for one employee depends on several factors, including but not limited to:

- Availability of talent in the marketplace. Jobs that are in high demand and low supply will cost more to recruit (e.g., advertising, recruiting services) and take longer to find a replacement. Incidentally, these jobs generally demand a higher salary.

- The higher the job level, the greater the costs to replace an employee. Generally, the greater the skill level, the longer and more expensive the recruiting process.

- The cost for those employees who leave involuntarily (i.e., fired) is generally greater than for those who leave voluntarily. When an employee is fired, the company may be required to pay out a severance package and other payments. The most expensive payments are given to executives. Frequently, executives have employment agreements with fat severance packages that require a *payout of hundreds of thousands to millions of dollars upon termination*. Ouch!

- Sign-on bonuses may be needed to hire a replacement.

- The time the position is left vacant impacts the costs. The longer the position is left open due to workload of those recruiting or difficulty in finding the right candidate, the greater the cost of turnover.

- Onboarding and training costs are greater for highly-technical jobs. They take longer to train because of the highly technical needs of the job. Plus, it takes longer for the new employees to become proficient at the job and reach full capacity.

- There is also the cost of lost opportunity, which is greatest in sales, marketing, and customer service jobs.

As you can see, there is a wide variety of costs, which are difficult to place a price tag on. Any way you calculate the costs of turnover, they are costs that you want to minimize to achieve competitive advantage. There are many ways to minimize these costs.

The Work Institute conducted an extensive seventeen-year study on why employees leave their jobs. This is reported in the *2017 Retention Report – Trends, Reasons and Recommendations* by Lindsay

Sears, Ph.D. The study involved interviewing 240,000 former employees to find out the real reasons they left their jobs. The Work Institute published the following top 10 reasons that employees left their jobs:

1. Career Development (22%): Opportunities for growth, achievement, and security

2. Work-Life Balance (12%): Travel and scheduling preferences

3. Management Behavior (11%): Positive and productive relationships

4. Compensation & Benefits (9%): Total rewards promised and received

5. Well-being (9%): Physical, emotional, and family-related issues

6. Retirement (8%)

7. Involuntary (8%)

8. Relocation (8%)

9. Job Characteristics (7%): Ownership and enjoyment in manageable work

10. Work Environment (6%): Physical and cultural surroundings

The good news is that most of these reasons are largely preventable, meaning that companies can shore up the areas that are leaking. I'm not saying that the leaks can be completely closed, but the leakage can be significantly reduced.

The Work Institute emphasizes the importance of knowing the unique needs of your workforce. Their research found that while there are common reasons across companies for turnover, the mix of reasons and priority of those reasons for each company they studied was different. For example, the top three reasons for companies A and B might look like this:

Company A

1. Work-Life Balance

2. Career Development

3. Well-being

Company B

1. Career Development

2. Job Characteristics

3. Management Behavior

Therefore, effective retention strategies for Company A and Company B would be different.

What this means for you is that you need to dig in and understand your workforce. Identify the real reasons employees leave your company and where the opportunities lie for you to reduce your turnover costs. Then create and implement your strategies. Don't just take these top 10 reasons and start implementing programs. *The Work Institute's top 10 reasons is a good place to start in uncovering the underlying problems.*

Further, The Work Institute reports that making even small investments in the areas where a company is lacking can have a big impact on the company. In the study, they give an example of a company that invests $100,000 in retention strategies. Assuming a very conservative turnover cost of $15,000, retaining just seven employees would pay for the investment. When you consider implementing new programs in your company, make sure that you are looking at the *return on investment* – not just the investment.

The Work Institute's study concludes, "Being able to contain turnover costs is not only a

> Being able to contain turnover costs is not only a competitive advantage, it is now necessary in today's employee marketplace to retain profits.

competitive advantage, it is now necessary in today's employee marketplace to retain profits." (Sears, 2017)

Hopefully, by now you are convinced that employees are truly your greatest asset, and you need to make people management part of your overall business strategy. So, where do you start? It all starts with leadership.

CHAPTER 4

Characteristics of a Magnetic Leader

IT TAKES A CERTAIN KIND of leader to create an engaged workforce. I call these people "Magnetic Leaders." These leaders walk the talk, and expect more of themselves than they do of others. They lead by example, and they are respected and trusted by their employees—not because these things are demanded by the leader, but because they are *earned*.

In Zig Ziglar's book *Born to Win*, he gives six personal qualities that are the "foundational stones" of success: honesty, character, love, loyalty, integrity and faith. I believe that they are also foundational qualities of a Magnetic Leader.

Foundational Stones of Success

Foundational qualities of a Magnetic Leader

Zig explains that these foundational stones provide the basis for making the right decisions that ultimately lead to sustained success. He says that success is found inside the person, not in the job. **Many people think that having a fancy degree(s) gives them a foundation for career success, but it is a person's character that ultimately determines how far he or she will go.**

I love what Jack Welch says about integrity in his book *Winning*,

…integrity is just a ticket to the game. If you don't have it in your bones, you shouldn't be allowed to play.

(Welch, 2005)

I've seen many bright and well-educated people come into our company only to be let go later due to a character flaw(s). What a waste of talent! I also know people who have thriving businesses who do not have a college degree, but they have good character. You see, being a Magnetic Leader starts with having a heart for people and the willingness to do the right thing.

Charlie Wingett, Scandipharm's founder whom I referenced earlier, was someone who modeled these foundational stones. One year, the company did not meet its revenue numbers, and the board of directors would not give the employees even a partial bonus for the year. Charlie felt so badly about this that he gave some of his *personal stock* in the company to each employee! That act of generosity had a profound effect on me and my view of leadership. Now, I'm not suggesting that leaders give away their personal stock. I use this example to show the heart of a Magnetic Leader.

Magnetic Leaders can be found at all levels of the company. Beyond the foundational stones described above, here are some other characteristics such leaders have in common:

- They have the *courage* to do the right thing in all circumstances.

- They are *genuine* and *authentic*.

- They have an attitude of *gratitude*.

- They see the big picture and think strategically.

- They are able to find the root causes of problems, instead of just looking at the symptoms, and they create effective solutions.

- They are able to create and communicate the vision for their company or area.

- They are excellent *two-way* communicators; they give and receive information well.

Magnetic Leaders are the ones who stand the tests of time. We've all seen those leaders who fly high for a while, then a scandal takes them down. These are the cheaters in life, those who only think of themselves and hurt other people. Ultimately, it catches up with them. No matter how much success they achieved initially, they lose it all.

> **"He who walks with integrity walks securely,**
> **but he who perverts his ways will become known."**
> — Proverbs 10:9

We had one of those scandals where I live (Birmingham, Alabama) that rocked the financial world in the early 2000s – the $2.8 billion accounting scandal at HealthSouth. Incidentally, Health-South offices were located only about a half-mile from Scandipharm. HealthSouth is a healthcare company that had phenomenal success and grew quickly to a Fortune 500 company within ten years. The company was founded and led by Richard Scrushy, who is widely known for his greed, lies, mistreatment of employees, and selfishness. Scrushy demanded that company employees falsely report grossly exaggerated company earnings in order to meet stockholder expectation and control the price of company stock. Scrushy sold a large amount of personal stock right before HealthSouth reported a loss in 2002. The SEC (U.S. Security and Exchange Commission) caught up with him, and the accounting fraud was revealed. In the end, Richard Scrushy went to jail and was ordered to pay HealthSouth $2.9 billion in restitution. Clearly, Scrushy was not a Magnetic Leader and did not have long-term success.

Zig Ziglar said,

> **"Ability can take you to the top,**
> **but it takes character to keep you there."**
> (ZIGLAR Z., 1990)

This is proven true time and time again. As I'm writing this book, there are numerous sexual harassment allegations against politicians and media leaders. Most of these allegations took place in the distant past. Women have been afraid to speak out against these powerful men, but some women found the courage and it has been a snowball effect. Currently, media moguls are dropping like flies as they are fired for sexual misconduct, and politicians are being disgraced. It is a shocking time as people who were formerly respected are having their true characters revealed.

As my mama always told me, "You reap what you sow." I want to encourage you to sow good seeds every day, so that you will receive a rich harvest of lasting success in your work and personal life.

CHAPTER 5

How to Become a Magnetic Leader

BASED ON THE CHARACTERISTICS DISCUSSED in the previous chapter, being a Magnetic Leader probably sounds like a tall order for anyone. However, I believe that most leaders with a *strong moral compass* can acquire a majority of the qualities. Zig Ziglar said,

> "You were born to win, but to be the winner you were born to be, you must plan to win and prepare to win.
> Then and only then can you expect to win."
> (ZIGLAR, 2012)

How do you plan and prepare to be a Magnetic Leader? First, you must have the willingness to commit to your own personal development on an ongoing basis. Tom Ziglar says, "Change starts with you, but it doesn't start until you do." (Ziglar, 2012) Being a Magnetic Leader starts on the inside of a person – at his or her very core.

SET DEVELOPMENT GOALS

To determine a course of action, assess your strengths and weaknesses. I've created a simple chart using the foundational qualities of a Magnetic Leader. This chart is available for download on my website paschakelley.com. Beside each quality, indicate whether each one is a strength or a weakness for you. The last column can be used to make notes related to your answer and ideas for development.

	Strength	Weakness	Notes
Honesty			
Character			
Faith			
Integrity			
Love			
Loyalty			
Courage			
Genuine/Authentic			
Grateful			
Strategic Thinker			
Problem Solver			
Visionary			
Excellent Communicator			

Engaging Leader assessment chart

First, look at all of your strengths. You probably have a nice list. Reviewing your strengths gives you encouragement. If you only look at your weaknesses, it is easy to get discouraged. Also, you can leverage your strengths to build up or overcome your weak areas.

Now, for your weaknesses. Check out the list and think of ways that you can create long-term improvement in those areas. In the next sections, I'll discuss two of the most important ways to develop your leadership skills: Mental Input and Community.

MENTAL INPUT

Your mental input determines how you think, influences your view of the world, and impacts your emotions and your actions. Research has found that mental input even affects our physical health. We receive input in many different ways. The primary categories are reading, watching, and listening; our community (e.g., family, friends, work associates, coaches) also provides input.

In this age of technology, we've become inundated with input, some good and a lot bad. The opportunity to develop the qualities of a Magnetic Leader involves selecting the right input and blocking out the bad. Zig Ziglar said,

> "You are what you are and where you are because of what has gone into your mind, but you can change what you are and where you are by changing what goes into your mind."
>
> (ZIGLAR, 2012)

To be a Magnetic Leader, you must be willing to expand your mind and constantly grow. Zig Ziglar read a minimum of three hours a day, and he took speed reading classes to be able to consume more information. Charlie Wingett not only read leadership books, he shared them with other people. When Charlie found a business book that he really liked, he would give a copy to all of his employees.

Even a small amount of reading each day is beneficial. I find that it helps to block off a certain time each day for personal development. Currently, I have several hours blocked out each morning for personal development. However, that wasn't always the case.

When I was a working mother in the corporate world, it was next to impossible to find time to read. This is when I started searching for other ways to learn while juggling responsibilities.

I discovered that I could listen to audiobooks while getting dressed in the morning. I particularly liked Joel Osteen audiobooks because they gave me encouragement and strength to face the day. I would listen to the same books over and over because I really needed that encouragement to just get through the day.

Eventually, I noticed that I was doing more than just making it through the day. My relationship with God was growing, and I was being shaped into a better person. Also, I started encouraging others with what I was learning. I'm a natural encourager, but filling my mind with encouragement brought my gift to a whole new level.

While driving to work and kids' activities, I listened to audiobooks from business leaders like Zig Ziglar, Stephen Covey, and Dave Ramsey. Zig called this form of learning "automobile university." Instead of focusing on the frustration of traffic, I was using that time to improve my skills and the way that I think.

I love to read, but I simply do not have time to sit down and read all of the books that I want to read. Listening to audio books gives me the opportunity to "read" those books while doing other things. Now that my kids can drive themselves and I work from home, I still listen to tons of audiobooks. However, now I listen to them on my iPhone while getting dressed, exercising, and working around the house.

I eventually learned about podcasts, which are FREE, and they opened up a whole new world of learning for me. The great thing about podcasts is that the information is current and forward- thinking. I've learned a lot about internet marketing and personal development from podcasts. I even learned about the Ziglar Legacy Certification program from the Ziglar podcast (my personal favorite), which launched a whole new career for me!

While there is a lot of good information on many podcasts, not every podcast is beneficial. Remember, anyone can do a podcast, and it is reflective of only one person or one group's opinion. So, you need to be careful about which podcasts you listen to. You can also pick and choose which episodes to listen to. You don't need to listen to all the podcasts from a certain person. I find that it is good to listen to podcasts from several different people to get the most balanced information.

I'm actually a visual learner – not an audio learner. However, I still learn a lot from audiobooks and podcasts. I may not catch every word they say, but I can always go back and listen to them again. I think that it is better to learn something instead of nothing at all.

Now that I work from home and my children are older, I have more time for learning. I start my day with a cup of coffee while watching Joyce Meyer on TV. You see, I'm NOT a morning person. I really need encouragement (and a lot of coffee) in the morning, and Joyce gives me that, plus a swift kick in the pants to get moving!

Joyce also teaches core competencies on how to be a Magnetic Leader. She doesn't call it that, but the majority of what she teaches strengthens my foundational stones. Listening to Joyce also helps me draw closer to my true source for success, which is God.

Now that I'm a speaker, I also watch Joyce to learn about her teaching and speaking style. Why do hundreds of thousands of people tune into her TV broadcasts and attend her conferences to see her speak? I want to figure that out so that I can be a great speaker too.

Finally, the woman is currently 74 years old! Despite having cancer and two hip replacement surgeries, she is still making an impact around the world with her teachings. She also seems to get better looking every year. How does she do that? Joyce places an emphasis on her personal health and fitness. She walks five miles a day and works out with weights 3 times a week. She also watches what she eats. Joyce is my role model for getting older!

Now, I know that Joyce Meyer is not everyone's cup of tea, which is perfectly fine. In fact, my husband tries to get up before me so that he can have control of the TV first because he doesn't like watching Joyce. However, he does appreciate that I watch her program, because it makes me a better person.

I use this example of watching Joyce Meyer in the morning to show how I constantly develop myself. I found something that works for me, and I've made it part of my morning routine. I record her shows so I can watch them at my convenience and re-watch them if needed (I am very sleepy in the morning). When I'm traveling, I can watch her shows on my laptop.

I encourage you to find ways to learn that fit into your lifestyle so you can adopt them as habits. I have found that if I try to force something into my schedule that doesn't work for me, I won't do it for long, and I don't benefit from it. As an example, my church has a powerful event twice a year called *21 Days of Prayer*. This involves having prayer meetings at 6:00 a.m. on weekdays. My husband and friends who attend receive great benefit from the prayer meetings. I've tried to go to these prayer meetings at 6:00 a.m., but it just resulted in me being irritable for the rest of the day. Additionally, I felt guilty that I hated going, which is the opposite of the intent of those prayer meetings. (Note: my church doesn't condemn people for not going – it is simply an opportunity for growth. The guilt came from me.)

While the church's prayer meetings are great for a lot of people, the timing goes against my very nature and doesn't provide benefit to me. Plus, I have my own time of spiritual growth each morning that works well for me. After I watch Joyce, I read my Bible, pray, and plan my day. *Trying to implement something that worked for other people, but not me, threw off my daily time of spiritual growth.*

Be careful of trying to fit into someone else's mold for your personal development. Just because something works for other people does not mean that it will work for you. Zig Ziglar said,

---

"Success is not measured by what you do compared to what others do. Success is measured by what you do compared to what you could have done with the ability God gave you."

(ZIGLAR Z., 2009)

You are unique! God created us all differently, and our schedules are different too. In this day and age, there are a multitude of ways to develop yourself. In addition to the ways listed above, there are online classes, webinars, and many other ways to learn. Find what works for YOU and incorporate it into your daily life. Make it a habit!

YOUR COMMUNITY

> You're the average of the five people
> you spend the most time with.
> — JIM ROHN (GROTH, 2012)

For purposes of this book, "community" means the people with whom you interact on a regular basis. It includes your family, friends, work associates, mentors, coaches, and people in groups in which you are involved. Some people you choose to be around; others you are forced to associate with.

First, let's look at those you place in your community. To be a Magnetic Leader, you need a lot of support. Surround yourself with people who are encouragers and mentors, who understand your dreams, and will help you accomplish them. You have to be intentional about finding these people. They are truly gems.

I've found those gems at Ziglar, Inc. What an amazing group of encouragers and leaders! Even though I do not work in the corporate office in Dallas, I am encouraged through weekly video meetings, emails, and social media. Plus, Julie Ziglar Norman, Zig's daughter, is my personal mentor, and I can call her when I need encouragement and guidance. Julie's personality is a lot like her dad's personality – upbeat and positive. I can't help but smile the whole time that I'm talking to her, and I always feel better after speaking with her.

A lot of people have asked me why I chose the Ziglar speaker program over other larger programs. I simply tell them that is where God led me. I investigated a lot of speaker programs, but I just knew deep down that I was supposed to go to Ziglar. And I'm so glad that I did! Being part of the close-knit Ziglar community is an incredible blessing to me.

While going through Ziglar training, I met Howard Partridge and learned about his small-business coaching program called Inner Circle. I joined immediately because I knew that I needed coaching, support, and encouragement to make my new business successful.

Howard gave me a personal coach, Rick Jones, who had previously worked with Dale Carnegie Training for thirty-five years. In fact, he built the Dale Carnegie business in Houston. Rick is an incredible coach! It seems like every time he opens his mouth, wisdom comes out. He is also a caring person with good character.

The Inner Circle also provides me with online resources, and the ability to ask questions and get answers quickly from one of the coaches. Howard provides weekly training via webinar on Tuesdays. The following day, I meet with my small group via video, which is led by Rick, to discuss the lesson. It is a solid coaching program. If you want to learn more about it, go to howardpartridgeinnercircle.com.

When looking for your personal coaches and mentors, look for these seven characteristics (Ziglar, 2012):

1.   They have **good character**.

2.   They have a **good track record of success**.

3.   They are **good listeners**.

4.   They are **good decision makers**.

5.   They **tell the truth** (even when it hurts).

6.   They have **good personal relationships**.

7.   They **celebrate the success of others**.

At the same time, you need to get away from people who complain, have bad attitudes, and bring you down. These people generally have lives that are a mess, and they want you to roll around in the pigpen with them. Zig would say these people have "stinkin' thinkin'" and need a "check-up from the neck up!"

Remember, you don't have to keep these negative people happy by continuing to be their friend or in their circle of influence. These stinkers are hindering your ability to be a Magnetic Leader. Further, you are not responsible for them (unless they are family), so carefully slip away from their clutches.

Now, there are some of these life-suckers with whom we have to work and live. The situation is what it is. When I'm dealing with these kinds of people, I limit my interaction with them as much as possible and try to put more good in my mind than the negative that they spew out.

I also ask for God's protection and read a lot of Psalms. This book of the Bible is my go-to when haters are after me, because it talks of trials and God's deliverance from those trials. I think of it as building an invisible barrier between that person and me so they can't drag me down.

While you can't choose everyone in your environment, when you can – choose well! Surround yourself with people who will build you up and help you achieve your dreams.

MAGNETIC CULTURE

Build the foundation
of a great culture
and bring it to life

CHAPTER 6

Culture Defined

EVERY COMPANY HAS A CULTURE. You can feel it when you walk in the doors – or maybe you heard about the culture before you even entered the doors. A company's culture is its personality. It is created by:

- Leadership styles

- Guiding principles and goals – or lack thereof

- Attitudes of the workforce

- Company policies and procedures

- What is considered "acceptable" and "unacceptable" behavior

- Work environment

Some companies have good cultures, and some have bad cultures. Culture creates a feeling, which is not easily described. When someone talks about a company's culture, he or she generally places it in either the "good" or the "bad" category.

I want to introduce you to another culture term: **Magnetic Culture**. This type of culture is specifically designed to attract, retain, and engage employees. I use the word "magnetic" because this is what the culture felt like at Scandipharm. It was the culture that attracted me to the company and held me there for so long.

A Magnetic Culture is a powerful tool for creating competitive advantage. It attracts the right people and ejects those who are wrong for the company. A Magnetic Culture motivates employees to do their best and go the extra mile. It retains employees, which reduces turnover costs. Overall, employees are engaged, customers are more satisfied, costs are reduced, and the company is more profitable. I think that Peter Drucker, the late business management expert, said it best: "Culture eats strategy for breakfast." (Hyken, 2015)

Several studies show that overcompensating an employee will not make up for a bad work environment. Companies who think they can engage and retain their employees by simply throwing money at them are wrong. Employers who grab their employees' hearts through creating a Magnetic Culture and wisely utilizing their resources will get ahead of the pack.

POWERFUL ATTRACTION

A magnet is an object that creates a force field; an invisible force that pulls other items to it. In the same way, when a company has a Magnetic Culture, people are drawn to that company. In fact, people line up to apply for jobs with the company. It is generally not because the magnetic company pays more. It is because it has something special of which people want to be a part.

With a lot of people wanting to work for the company, it can select the best and brightest in the group. This gives the magnetic company competitive advantage because it gets the pick of the litter.

Richard Branson explains it like this:

Create the kind of workplace and company culture
that will attract great talent. If you hire brilliant people,
they will make work feel more like play.

(ROBERTS, 2015)

For examples of companies with a Magnetic Culture, check out the "Best Places to Work" lists. These companies are intentional about creating an environment where people want to work.

HOLDING POWER

Companies with a Magnetic Culture have highly-engaged workforces who are committed to the company. Therefore, magnetic companies hold people. Not literally, but they do hold the employees' hearts and commitment. This lowers the high cost of employee turnover, which boosts profits.

PULLS TOGETHER

A Magnetic Culture pulls people together instead of pushing them apart. This culture encourages teamwork and expels those who hurt the team.

WHAT DOES A MAGNETIC CULTURE LOOK LIKE?

A Magnetic Culture makes employees feel like they are part of a family, and their work place is like a second home where they work hard, but that work is appreciated. They are recognized for their contributions to their company. There is also some fun involved, and friendships develop.

The employees at a magnetic company worry less about their families and other responsibilities outside of work because they are given the freedom to produce great work while taking care of those they love. They also have resources like employee assistance plans and stress reduction education to help them better manage these responsibilities.

Bosses in a magnetic company provide clear and effective communications. They establish goals and help employees achieve them. They care about their people.

You can tell a company with a Magnetic Culture because it is apparent in their business. The customer service is better, and employees are simply happier. After all, employees treat customers the way they are treated, no matter what kind of training they have had and what kind of incentives are in place. Steven Covey said, "**Always treat your employees exactly as you want them to treat your best customers**." (Hakobyan, 2016) If a person is miserable in his or her job, it will reflect in his or her performance.

Zappos is a company that is known for its good culture. Tony Hsieh, CEO of Zappos, says,

> Our number-one priority is company culture. Our belief is that if you get the culture right, most of the other stuff like delivering great customer service or building a great long-term brand will happen naturally on its own.
>
> (BULYGO, 2013)

MY EXPERIENCE

I personally learned about working for a magnetic company in my early twenties. At Scandipharm, our visionary founder, Charlie Wingett, implemented the principles of the book *Built to Last* in our company. *Built to Last: Successful Habits of Visionary Companies* is a book by Jim Collins and Jerry Porras. The book is based on the results of a six-year research project at the Stanford University Graduate School of Business. They studied 18 companies that had an average age of 100 years and outperformed the stock market by a factor of 15 since 1926. The authors researched what made those companies different from other companies. The results of the study were placed into this book, and thanks to Charlie, the success factors were implemented into our company.

Charlie started by giving every employee a copy of the *Built to Last* book. In fact, I still have the memo from 1996 he wrote that accompanied the book. (For young folks, "memos" are how we communicated in offices before email.) Charlie brought in a consultant to lead the effort. We had off-site meetings where everyone participated in building our mission, vision, purpose, and core values statements. Thus, I felt ownership of those values.

Experiencing the creation of our company's guiding principles had a huge impact on me personally. When I talk about creating a Magnetic Culture, this is not just something that I've read in a book. I've lived it!

CHAPTER 7

How to Create a Magnetic Culture

There's no magic formula for great company culture. The key is just to treat your staff how you would like to be treated.

— RICHARD BRANSON (VIRGIN.COM)

TO CREATE A MAGNETIC CULTURE, you first have to determine what the company stands for and where it is going. Zig Ziglar said, "All of us perform better and more willingly when we know why we're doing what we have been told or asked to do." (Ziglar Z. , 1990)

The starting point is creating your guiding principles: vision statement, mission statement and core values. These guiding principles are the building blocks of a Magnetic Culture. Each statement serves a different purpose in developing the company's unique culture.

All of us perform better and more willingly when we know why we're doing what we have been told or asked to do.

— ZIG ZIGLAR

VISION STATEMENT

Where there is no vision, the people perish.

— PROVERBS 29:18

The vision statement is the desired future state of the company. It provides direction, inspiration, and hope. The vision statement should create a mental picture of the desired state of the company.

Proverbs 29:18 says, "Where there is no vision, the people perish." To create a Magnetic Culture, your people need a vision. As stated in the section on Employee Engagement, the Dale Carnegie study found that Inspired is one of the four traits of an engaged employee.

In Howard Partridge's book *The 5 Secrets of a Phenomenal Business*, he states that his business slogan is "Inspiration to Implementation." Howard is one of my coaches, and I can tell you that he is one of the most inspirational people I know! He says that the most successful business owners are those who are excited about the future. *These people are not inspired because they are growing. They are growing because they are inspired.*

The ability to effectively share the company's vision is one of the most important leadership skills a person needs to possess to lead a company. This does not mean that the leader has to have charisma. Charlie Wingett was not a charismatic leader. Charlie was soft-spoken, but he was able to share his vision and motivate people to achieve that vision. Charlie also made sure that the core values were woven into the fabric of our company, which I will address later in this book.

Here are some examples of vision statements:

- **Disney**—To make people happy.

- **Ikea**—To create a better everyday life for the many people.

- **Microsoft**—Empower every person and every organization on the planet to achieve more.

- **Ford**—People working together as a lean, global enterprise to make people's lives better through automotive and mobility leadership.

A vision statement can evolve over time as your company and the environment changes. Zig Ziglar said, "The basic goal-reaching principle is to understand that you go as far as you can see, and when you get there you will always be able to see farther." (Ziglar Z. , 1990) Don't allow fear of not being able to predict the future prevent you from creating a vision statement. Based on what you know at this time, create a vision statement that will provide direction and inspiration to your company.

MISSION STATEMENT

A mission statement describes *why* a company exists. It supports the vision statement. It also helps you stay focused on what your company is about. When business opportunities become available, you should measure them against your mission statement. If you get too spread out, you won't be as effective.

A mission statement is key to creating a Magnetic Culture in that it defines the purpose of the company. Employees need to understand the company's purpose in order to be committed to achieving it. Jack Welch, the legendary CEO of General Electric, sees having a mission statement as key to long-term success. He said,

There are only three measurements that tell you nearly everything you need to know about your organization's overall performance: employee engagement, customer satisfaction, and cash flow. It goes without saying that no company, small or large, can win over the long run without energized employees who believe in the mission and understand how to achieve it.

(WINDUST, 2015)

A Dale Carnegie Training study identified three key drivers for employee engagement.

1.　　Relationship with direct manager

2.　　Belief in senior leadership

3.　　*Pride in working for the company*

Today's workforce wants to know that they are working for more than a paycheck. They want to have lives of significance. They want to make a difference in their communities and the world. A company's mission statement helps give employees a sense of purpose.

TOMS shoe company is a great example of a company that was built with a clear purpose. The initial business model was buy a pair of shoes, and one would be given to a child in need. The company's founder, Blake Mycoskie, started the company to fund his giving to children in South America. Mycoskie says that TOMS was not a company with a mission. It was a mission that turned into a company.

> **When people are financially invested, they want a return. When people are emotionally invested, they want to contribute.**
>
> —SIMON SINEK

Simon Sinek said, "When people are financially invested, they want a return. When people are emotionally invested, they want to contribute." (Windust, 2015) This is the power of the mission statement. It helps rally people around a common cause.

Scandipharm's mission was *to improve the quality of care and treatment of patients suffering from gastrointestinal diseases and related disorders by providing effective therapies, products, and specialized programs that meet the needs of these patients and their caregivers.*

Now, this mission statement was a bit long and not easily understood (it was originally created in the 1990s), so I'm not promoting it as a great example of a mission statement. I think that a mission statement should be easy for anyone to read and understand. However, I wanted you to see this mission statement so I can share an important part of the culture developed around this statement. At Scandipharm, we had a huge "Why We Work" corkboard that held pictures of patients and their thank-you letters. This board was placed where everyone could see it, and it helped drive the mission statement home. It gave the employees the feeling that what they did at work every day mattered.

Also, in line with our mission statement, Scandipharm and its employees were involved in efforts to raise money for the Cystic Fibrosis (CF) Foundation. The company's primary focus was providing medications and services for CF patients. Our employees participated annually in the CF Great Strides walk to raise money to cure CF and improve the lives of those with the disease. Being involved in the CF community was an important part of our culture that was tied to the mission statement.

Here are some examples of other companies' mission statements:

- **Amazon**—We strive to offer our customers the lowest possible prices, the best available selection, and the utmost convenience.

- **Google**—To organize the world's information and make it universally accessible and useful.

- **Jet Blue**—JetBlue's mission is to inspire humanity – both in the air and on the ground. We are committed to giving back in meaningful ways in the communities we serve and to inspire others to do the same.

- **Publix Super Markets**—Our mission at Publix is to be the premier quality food retailer in the world.

If you do not have a mission statement already, I encourage you to create one. Write it down, and share it with your people. Better yet, get your people involved in creating a mission statement.

Once you have a mission statement, I encourage you to bring it to life. Make it more than words on a page. If you serve customers, share with your employees how they make a difference in people's lives. Your employees need this! They need to know that their work matters.

CORE VALUES

Core Values are the company's deeply-held beliefs. They serve as the company's guiding principles and basis for decision-making. Core Values are simple, clear, straightforward statements. They are *internal* drivers and are not affected by changes in the outside environment. Core Values are a solid foundation for the company and do not sway with the trends of the day. In fact, they help companies through change.

Typically, a company has only three to six Core Values. These values are so deeply held and unchanging that only a small number are needed. To develop Core Values, you can get ideas from other companies; however, you should never *copy* another company's Core Values. They have to be unique to your company and your beliefs. Developing Core Values is not a calculated process and should not be influenced by what the outside world thinks they should be.

When we developed our Core Values and other guiding principles at Scandipharm, we went to an off-site conference center in the woods. We had an outside consultant facilitate the process (although, this is not necessary). Scandipharm was tight on money at this time, so the fact that money was being spent on an off-site meeting and a consultant sent a message to me that this was serious business.

The entire company was involved for one day in the creation process of our guiding principles. Management stayed for an additional day to finalize the statements. Because I was involved in this process, the company's guiding principles were very personal to me. It was the same for others who were part of the process. Dale Carnegie said, "People help support a world they helped create" (dalecarneggie.com), and I have found that to be true.

I think that involving a lot of people in the creation process of those values created a kind of virus effect as the company grew. As new employees were hired, the originators of those values spread the enthusiasm and passion they felt about the values. I had many people tell me that they could see my passion about those values, and it made them feel passionate about them as well.

I highly recommend involving as many employees as you can in the development process of your Core Values and other guiding statements. Warren G. Bennis, who was known as the Father of Leadership, said:

Good leaders make people feel that they're at the very heart of things, not at the periphery. Everyone feels that he or she makes a difference to the success of the organization. When that happens, people feel centered, and that gives their work meaning.

(WINDUST, 2015)

Sadly, in 1997, we lost Charlie (age 55) to a heart attack. Our company went through many changes after that time. We had some good leaders and some bad leaders; mergers and acquisitions; and wins and losses. However, I always felt that the core values gave us roots to withstand the many challenges that we faced later. Charlie left a rich legacy and an indelible mark on my life as a leader.

CHAPTER 8

Integration into Fabric of the Company

FOR THESE GUIDING STATEMENTS TO be effective, they have to be woven into the fabric of the company. This requires taking the Vision, Mission, Core Values, and any other guiding principles, and translating them into action. In *Built to Last*, this is described as follows:

> ...visionary companies translate their ideologies into tangible mechanisms aligned to send a consistent set of reinforcing signals. They indoctrinate people, impose tightness of fit, and create a sense of belonging to something special through practical concrete items.
>
> (COLLINS, 1994)

Lack of integration is where many companies are missing the mark. After the corporate scandals of the early 2000s, there was a rush for companies to make themselves look trustworthy. This usually involved leaders creating Core Values and other guiding principles in a meeting, or having an outside consultant create the "appropriate" statements for them. Leaders would announce to the employees and the world that they had created these wonderful guiding statements, and that they were committed to them.

This is all well and good, but for some companies, it was just putting paint on a dilapidated building. Due to the sense of urgency around making companies look trustworthy, many leaders created guiding principles from a sense of necessity, not from their core beliefs. For leaders who didn't understand the importance of having guiding principles or were just lacking in character, they simply met the PR obligations and went on their way. That's it! The principles were not implemented in the company.

LEADERS: If you create a set of values and do not demonstrate them, you are doing more harm than good. Do not create Core Values and other guiding principles if you are not going to model them.

While I've seen great leaders create and demonstrate Core Values, I've also seen leaders who give lip-service to the company's values, then turn around and do something completely contrary to those values. *Do you trust someone who is two-faced?* Neither do employees. They won't follow, respect, nor stay with a leader who says one thing and does another. Also, word gets around to potential employees, and they don't want to work there either.

In John Maxwell's book *The 21 Irrefutable Laws of Leadership*, he says, **"Trust is the foundation of leadership."** (Maxwell, 1998 and 2007) If a leader continuously breaks people's trust, he can't influence them. It takes an authentic leader to build and maintain that trust.

Frances Hesselbein, founder of the Leadership Institute, said:

Culture does not change because we desire to change it. Culture changes when the organization is transformed; the culture reflects the realities of people working together every day.

(HESSELBEIN, SPRING 1999)

Culture is something that you simply can't fake. If you want to create a Magnetic Culture, you must integrate the guiding principles throughout the company, and most importantly, model those behaviors yourself!

There are many ways to integrate your guiding principles throughout your company to create a Magnetic Culture. In the next sections, I will share several ways to bring your guiding principles to life and embed them in the fabric of your company.

CHAPTER 9

Hiring Process

There's a world of potential teammates out there.
The culture you create determines who you attract,
so craft it carefully to hire the inspired.

— ROBYN BENINCASA (DRYSDALE, 2017)

COMPETITION FOR SKILLED WORKERS IS growing fierce. A large segment of the population is retiring, and there are not enough skilled workers to take their places. Additionally, job growth is expected to increase while the talent pool shrinks. These conditions give skilled workers the power to be more selective about where they work.

People want to work for companies that have a reputation for maintaining a good culture. Let's face it, we spend most of our lives at work. People have figured out that the workplace can actually be enjoyable, and companies who provide this are magnets for employees. There are studies, like *Fortune's* "The 100 Best Companies to Work For," that describe what the best companies are providing for their employees. You can bet that there is a line of applicants for all of these companies.

Many local magazines/organizations recognize companies in the community that are great to work for. In my city, the *Birmingham Business Journal* (BBJ) provides an annual "Best Places to Work" contest and publishes the winners. The winners are determined by an employee survey, and winners are the top scorers in their size categories. **The BBJ states, "…the common thread between all 35 companies the BBJ recently named Birmingham's Best Places to Work was culture. Each of the honorees has created a unique culture where employees feel valued and workers remain engaged."** (Ty West, 2016)

Do you think a company that is listed as a best place to work has problems recruiting top talent and retaining them? No, people flock to these companies and are not easily picked off by other companies. *What do you think this does to their bottom line and ability to compete in their industry?* I can tell you that none of the companies on the "Best of" lists are struggling to make a profit.

When you post job openings in your company, make sure that you are very specific about the type of person who would successfully fit into your culture. In *EntreLeadership*, Dave Ramsey provides examples of how his culture is described in ads:

- "Just because your mother likes your family blog doesn't make you a writer; you really must have professional writing experience,

- Two years of sales experience needed, Girl Scout cookies doesn't count,

- We might be wearing blue jeans and flip-flops, but don't let that fool you, we work our tails off. If you want to join a team that gets it done then you better know how to make things happen." (Ramsey, 2011)

For some free advertising, try to get on the "Best Places to Work" list in your community, or the *Fortune* lists. Most of these lists are divided by size, so don't be intimidated if you have a small company. These businesses are recognized as well.

Also, don't forget your current employees. If they love their jobs, they will tell others. Your current employees can help you attract other great employees. Implementing an Employee Referral Program, where employees are rewarded for recommending qualified candidates, is a great way to find employees who are a good fit for your organization.

GET THE RIGHT PEOPLE ON THE BUS

If there is one thing that has helped me as a coach, it's my ability to recognize winners, or good people who can become winners by paying the price.
— COACH BEAR BRYANT (COOPER, 2012).

After completing his *Built to Last* project, Jim Collins embarked on a new study to find out how companies who did not have a good start (like the Built-to-Last companies) were able to make the leap from good to great and sustain those results for at least 15 years. In this study, he found key determinants for greatness – why those companies were able to make the leap and others were not. In his book *Good to Great*, Jim Collins details what he found from the study. I will discuss some of those principles here.

One of the key concepts of *Good to Great* is getting the right people on the bus and in the right seats, and getting the wrong people off the bus. When you have the right people on the bus:

- They are able to change direction easily when needed.
- They are internally motivated, so they do not need as much supervision.
- If you have the wrong people, it doesn't matter what the company's vision is, you won't be able to accomplish it.

Good-to-great companies have rigorous processes for managing people. Consistent standards are applied at all times and at all levels. The research identified three practical disciplines of the good-to-great companies:

1. **"When in doubt, don't hire – keep looking"**. Only the *right people* can create a great company. Don't settle for less. The *Harvard Business Review* estimates that 80% of employee turnover is due to bad hiring decisions. Take the time to find the right people up front.

2. **"When you know you need to make a people change – act**." If a person did not seem to be a good fit, good-to-great companies first assessed whether that person was in the wrong seat on the bus. If that wasn't the problem, they dismissed the person as soon as possible. Hanging on to the wrong people is unfair to the right people, and you don't want to lose them.

3. **"Put your best people on your biggest opportunities, not your biggest problems**." The best people should receive the best opportunities, not the worst problems.

When I talk about "rigorous processes" and "discipline," I'm not talking about the structure of the workplace environment. Having a free-flowing, happy environment is part of the rich corporate culture for many companies. However, when it comes to who you hire and who stays with the company, that process must be structured and administered with discipline. To maintain a thriving culture, you can't have snakes lurking around.

EJECT THOSE WHO DON'T FIT

Mediocre people don't like high achievers, and high achievers don't like mediocre people.
— COACH NICK SABAN (KETEYIAN, 2014).

Hiring the right people is tricky because people will say anything to get the job. If you find that you have hired someone who is not a good fit for your organization, you should get rid of them *fast*. One rotten apple can ruin the whole barrel. If you have someone in your organization who is not acting according to the core values, he or she is probably harming other people and hurting your culture. Don't hesitate – show that person the door!

At Zappos, they offer new employees $3,000 to quit after the initial training if they feel the job isn't right for them. This may seem like a waste of money, but it is actually an investment. It will cost the company more money if they allow an employee to stay who doesn't fit into the culture. Zappos basically cuts their losses on that employee early.

In *Built to Last,* it says, "Only those who 'fit' extremely well with the core ideology and demanding standards of a visionary company will find it a great place to work. If you go to work at a visionary company, you will either fit and flourish – probably couldn't be happier – or you will be expunged like a virus. It's binary. There's no middle ground. It's almost cult-like. Visionary companies are so clear about what they stand for and what they're trying to achieve that they simply don't have room for those unwilling or unable to fit their exacting standards." (Collins, 1994)

Visionary companies are so clear about what they stand for and what they're trying to achieve that they simply don't have room for those unwilling or unable to fit their exacting standards.

A company that is considered a "Best Place to Work" company is not the best place for everyone to work. The "Best Places to Work" companies generally require enthusiasm, commitment, hard work, and the ability to buy into the company's demanding culture. While these companies look great from the outside, not everyone can fit into the company culture.

In the *Built to Last* study, the authors found that visionary companies are not soft and undisciplined; quite the opposite. Since these companies are so focused, they are actually more demanding than other companies. After our doors closed at Scandipharm, employees went to other businesses. Now, when talking with my former colleagues from Scandipharm, they tell me how different work is at other companies. They don't have to work as hard at those companies, and they don't have to put in the long hours. We're amazed that there is another world out there. We were so caught up in the Scandipharm culture, we didn't realize that other people don't work like us!

ONBOARDING PROCESS

At Scandipharm, we had a room called the "War Room." It held symbols of our culture (e.g., wolf head, axe handles) and the oak kitchen table that our founder used as his desk to start the company. As part of the onboarding process, a senior executive would take the new employees into the War Room and tell them the history of our company. He would talk about our mission, vision, core values, and why we do what we do. This grabbed the new employees' hearts and helped integrate them into our culture.

During our Ziglar Legacy Certification training, Zig Ziglar's three children (Tom, Julie, and Cindy) shared personal stories about Zig and their family. They treated us like part of the Ziglar family, and we felt like a part of that family by the time we left training. They actually have a name for us – "Ziglets." People who go through this program say that it is life changing, and that they gain more than they expected.

From a practical standpoint, the company's guiding principles should be explained in the onboarding process. If you can create a way to make this an emotional experience, it will embed those values even deeper.

Also, the rewards of demonstrating core values and the consequences of not demonstrating those values should be discussed during the on-boarding process.

CHAPTER 10

Performance Management

WHAT GETS MEASURED GETS DONE. Most companies have a way to measure whether an employee has met his or her goals. However, most companies do not measure *how* those objectives are met. The *how* has a significant impact on the culture. If goals are being met in a way that does not align with the guiding principles of the company, then a conflict exists that takes the "magnetic pull" out of the culture.

You've probably worked with someone who is a high individual performer, but creates destruction on his or her way to success. This could be because of a lack of integrity, not working as a team, stepping on others on the way to the top, and generally creating a feeling of ill-will within the company. This type of behavior eventually impacts the company in terms of turnover, loss of engagement, and even law suits and fines. Therefore, it is very important to assess how the work is actually getting done.

The way you measure the *how* is by defining **behaviors** that are expected within the company, and by assessing whether the employee demonstrated those behaviors. These behaviors are also called "competencies." If you are an HR nerd like me, you probably know this as competency-based performance management program. However, to keep it simple, I'm going to just use the word "behavior" instead of "competency."

At Scandipharm, we developed a performance management program that measured both whether an employee met his annual objectives and the behaviors he demonstrated in achieving those objects. The behaviors measured were based on our Core Values. The final performance management score was based on *what* and *how* objectives were met.

When we added the behavior section to the existing performance management program, we expected pushback from managers. Let's face it, no one likes performance reviews, and we didn't think they would like more work in this area. However, the managers thanked us! The behavior measurement system gave them a tool to discuss problematic behaviors with their employees. They reported that the behavior system gave them the words to say during their talks with employees. Sometimes, it can be difficult to describe negative behaviors, and we made it easy for them. Go, HR! This behavior-based system also provided a vehicle for praising employees for the good behaviors they show and reinforcing those behaviors.

To really ramp up your program and help managers develop their people, create a training resource guide that provides development resources for each behavior. When a manager identifies a behavior issue, he or she can work with the employee to select training from that resource guide to shore up his or her weak area. This makes the manager's job easier and makes him or her more effective.

To create a behavior-based performance program, start by defining satisfactory behaviors for each Core Value. You can add behaviors for other guiding principles as well. How many behaviors you define is up to you. Then, define what unsatisfactory behavior and above-average behavior looks like. To help you get started, I've provided a template with instructions on my website paschakelley.com.

TIP: It is very helpful to define behaviors in a team, and it doesn't have to be only HR folks. It is actually better to get a mixed group of people from different departments and levels to define the behaviors.

As an example, I've created a behavior-based system for a company whose Core Values are Integrity, Customer Service, and Team Work. The supervisor reads the list of behaviors for each category and selects a score that best describes the employee's behavior.

	UNSATISFACTORY = 10 PTS.	SATISFACTORY = 20 PTS.	EXCEEDS EXPECTATIONS = 30 PTS.	SCORE
INTEGRITY	Does not maintain confidentiality; Gossips about other employees; Provides inaccurate or misleading information; Makes excuses instead of taking responsibility	Maintains confidentiality; Gives credit to other employees; Provides accurate information; Takes responsibility for mistakes	Recognized for being trustworthy; Attempts to provide most accurate picture; Provides solutions for mistakes	20
CUSTOMER SERVICE	Takes minimal action to understand customers' needs; Fails to quickly resolve customer concerns; Does not consistently follow through with customers	Effective in discovering customers' needs; Resolves customer concerns in a timely manner; Consistently follows through on commitments	Invests great energy to better understand the customers' needs; Follows up with customers to ensure the issue is resolved to their satisfaction; Excels in follow through with customers	10
TEAM WORK	Does not work well with others; Hinders productivity of team; Does not fulfill assignments in a timely manner or at all	Works well with others; Contributes to team and seeks input from others; Performs team duties assigned in a timely manner	Facilitates positive relationships within the team; Actively contributes to the team; Exceeds expectations on assignments	30
AVERAGE				20

Example of a behavior-based performance program

The behavior-based system does not have to be numerical. It can be scored as words: Unsatisfactory, Satisfactory, and Exceeds Expectations. However, when a program has a numerical score, it is easier to tie the performance score to compensation.

CHAPTER 11

Compensation and Recognition Programs

Compensation plans are like recognition: be careful to reward the activities you want duplicated. The team's activity will gravitate quickly toward how they get paid, so make sure to pay only for the things you want done

— DAVE RAMSEY (RAMSEY, 2011).

COMPENSATION

To integrate the guiding principles into your compensation plan, you must define your expectations and how those will be measured and rewarded. The easiest way to do this is through the behavior-based system described in the previous chapter or through a similar program.

The score from the behavior-based program can be used to make salary increase decisions, target promotion eligibility, and determine variable pay (bonus, commissions) amounts. **When you hit employee' pocketbooks, they stand up and take notice**. If you tie their behavior to their pay, they understand how important it is to adhere to the guiding principles of the company. I will discuss compensation in more detail in the next section.

RECOGNITION PROGRAMS

Companies with a Magnetic Culture celebrate achievements a lot! The accomplishments of individuals, teams, and the company are all recognized frequently. This gives people the feeling that they are part of a winning team, which makes them feel like winners. Also, corporate celebrations help bond people together as teammates in achieving goals.

> **Work is too much a part of life not to recognize moments of achievement. Grab as many as you can. Make a big deal out of them.**
> —JACK WELCH (WELCH, 2005)

People generally do not want to leave winning teams. In fact, studies show that turnover rates are lower at companies that are intentional with their recognition programs. In *The Carrot Principle,* a Watson Wyatt Reward Plan Survey was cited:

> **.... the average turnover rate of employers with clear reward strategy is 13% lower than that of organizations without one.**
> (ELTON, 2007, 2009),

Companies should celebrate big wins as well as milestones toward achieving objectives. While this is important during the good times, it is even more important during down times. Celebrating small victories when a company is struggling gives people hope and encourages them to keep going.

During the early years at Scandipharm, when we were such underdogs, our leaders celebrated those small successes (e.g., new high in revenue, completing a key project) with the whole company. Even though we had a long way to go to be able to play with the big dogs,

celebrating each tiny victory encouraged us to look at the possibilities instead of the obstacles.

At Zappos, "Deliver Wow" is one of their core values. To help re-inforce this, employees can give a $50 "coworker bonus award" when they catch someone delivering the Wow. Each employee can only give one coworker bonus award each month, but there is no limit to how many each employee can receive. This award serves two purposes: 1) it integrates Core Values, and 2) it provides *immediate* recognition to employees. Having a mechanism for on-the-spot rewards is key to having an effective recognition program.

Recognition programs are a powerful way to integrate the company's core values and build a Magnetic Culture. To do this, establish awards to recognize people who demonstrate the company's core values. I will discuss how to build a recognition program in the next section.

CHAPTER 12

Cultural Symbols

SYMBOLS REPRESENT THE COMPANY'S CULTURE in a tangible way. To create a Magnetic Culture, create unique symbols that inspire and motivate your employees. These symbols probably won't have meaning for people outside of your organization, which is actually a good thing. Cultural symbols make employees feel like insiders, which promotes a sense of togetherness.

As mentioned in the previous chapter, at Scandipharm, we had a War Room with the symbols of our struggles and victories. We had a mounted wolf head with his tongue hanging out that we called "Scandiwolf." The wolf was our company mascot. Our founder chose the wolf because of its pack mentality of working together toward a goal. He got this idea from a leadership book, *Wisdom of Wolves: Leadership Lessons from Nature*, by Twyman Towery.

In the War Room, we had axe handles hanging on the wall with teal ribbons hanging off of them. After a company setback, a marketing manager said in frustration that every time we start to peek our head out of the hole, someone comes along and smacks us back down with an axe handle. Those axe handles represented our struggle and determination not to be held back.

Each axe handle had a plaque engraved with the name of a department. During award ceremonies, employees were recognized for short-term accomplishments with teal ribbons which stated their achievements. The ribbons were then glued to the appropriate axe handles. So, the ribbons represented our accomplishments toward taking down the obstacles that stood in our way to success. By the way, the color teal was our corporate color. These axe handles engaged the employees and cost the company very little money.

At Ziglar, one of our symbols is the water pump. When I first arrived at Ziglar training, I was wondering, "What is the deal with the pump?" I found out that at Ziglar this symbol represents hard work and persistence that lead to success. It is based on one of Zig's most famous stories that goes something like this:

There were two ol' boys driving around in south Alabama on a hot August day. They became thirsty and pulled over to an old abandoned farmhouse. There was a pump sitting on top of a well. One of the boys grabbed the handle and started pumping. However, no water came out. The boys figured out that they needed to put water from a nearby creek into the pump to prime it

The boys primed the pump and kept pumping for several more minutes and still nothing came out. One of the boys was ready to give up, but the other reminded him that the wells are deep in south Alabama. This is good because the deeper the well, the cooler, the cleaner, the sweeter, and the better tasting the water.

One of the boys did give up and stopped pumping. The other grabbed the pump and kept pumping because he knew that the water would go back down the well and all of their effort would be for nothing. Finally, fresh, clean water came pouring out of the well.

Zig tells this story to teach several life lessons.

- We must put something in before we can get something out (prime the pump).

- The harder we work, the greater the reward.

- Anything worth doing is worth doing poorly until you can do it well.

- If you will pump long enough, hard enough, and enthusiastically enough, eventually you will receive the rewards.

When you walk into Ziglar headquarters, the first thing you see is Zig Ziglar's wall of gratitude. This is a wall with framed pictures of the people who have impacted his life. There is a plaque under each picture that gives the name of the person. There is Sister Jessie, who converted Zig to Christ. P.C. Merrill, who gave Zig his start in business. My personal favorite is Mary Kay Ash, who helped Zig publish his first book. You see, my mother was a Mary Kay Director, and Mary Kay insisted that they read Zig's books and listen to his audio cassettes. My mother's knowledge trickled down to me, and now I work with the Ziglar company. So, I am very grateful to Mary Kay!

The more you express gratitude for what you have, the more you will have to express gratitude for.
— ZIG ZIGLAR

The wall of gratitude makes a statement about what this company is about. It tells everyone who walks through those doors that gratitude is part of our culture. Even though Zig is no longer with us, he is still teaching us that we should be grateful. This was a part of his success, and it can be for us as well. It also says that entitlement is not allowed in this company. It is not acceptable behavior.

I first experienced the power of cultural symbols in my college sorority. Each sorority has symbols that represent their group. Some symbols are known to outsiders (e.g., Greek letters, colors), and others are secrets only known by the members. Revealing those secrets is part of the initiation process. The purpose of these symbols is to create a sense of togetherness and belonging. I was a Pi Beta Phi in college, and I wore my Greek letters proudly to show that I was part of that group. My daughter, Madeline, is in college now, and she is a Delta Gamma. Their symbol is the anchor, and I find myself buying all kinds of anchor stuff because I know that symbol is important to her.

Clubs and organizations use symbolism to unify their groups. To start creating symbolism in your company, think about the groups that you're involved in and how they use symbols to bind their members together. Now, think about your company's culture and how you can create symbols to represent it.

TIP: Get other people involved in the creation process. Find creative thinkers who have a natural gift for this type of thing. I call these people "Culture Builders." They are skilled at bringing the culture to life. Search these people out and employ them to help build your Magnetic Culture.

CHAPTER 13

Social Events

SOCIAL EVENTS ARE A KEY part of creating a Magnetic Culture. These events help employees develop friendships and camaraderie, and make employees feel like family. Enjoying social activities and celebrating special occasions create a sense of togetherness that is a big part of the culture.

I recommend having some social events where employees can bring their families. When you do something for people's children, you touch their hearts, which is key to creating engagement.

SOCIAL COMMITTEE

I suggest creating a social committee to make the magic happen. This committee should be comprised of the *fun people* in the office, who have as much fun planning events as being part of them. For the record, I'm not one of these people, so I have great appreciation for those who make our workplace fun.

> The social committee should be a group of Culture Builders, who will help you build and promote your Magnetic Culture.

The social committee should be a group of Culture Builders, who will help you build and promote your Magnetic Culture. The group should be diversified, representing the interests of most of your employees. You need to have a mix of women and men, various age groups, and departments. You also need people who are creative and willing to put in the extra effort to plan and execute great events.

The social committee should have a budget allocated to them for the expense of the events. The size of the budget will determine the number and type of events they plan for the year. Keep in mind that social events are a critical part of creating a rich corporate culture that creates engagement and retention. So, even though the events will cost you money initially, you will probably save more money in the long run. *Remember the high cost of employee turnover that we discussed in Section I?* **If the social events create the engagement needed to retain even one key employee, the savings could pay for the cost of events for the whole year!**

I recommend that the social committee create an events calendar for the entire year. At Scandipharm, our social committee planned a monthly event, which generally involved food. Down south we love to eat! In the fall, we had a chili cook-off, a pumpkin patch outing with families, and a Thanksgiving luncheon with a contest for best dish in each category. We also had a corporate event at a Birmingham Barron's baseball game in the spring where people could bring their families.

We had a children's Christmas party for the employees' kids, complete with Santa Clause and presents. My children looked forward to it every year. We also had a Christmas party for employees and their spouses at a nice venue. The ladies got to wear their party dresses, and there was a raffle for prizes. The party also involved some crazy dancing and karaoke. You don't really know your coworkers until you attend a Christmas party with them.

Our social committee also planned the awards ceremonies. Leadership selected the award winners. However, the social committee planned a fun event around the ceremony. These ceremonies were usually in conjunction with a social event.

After the first full year, planning social events gets a bit easier. The events that are successful can be repeated each year and become traditions that employees look forward to.

TIP: The company president or other leader should always recognize and thank the social committee members at the end of an event for a job well-done. While serving on the committee doesn't need to be a paid position, Scandipharm gave the social committee a nice gift certificate or cash at the Christmas party each year. These people didn't serve on the committee for money, but the gift was always appreciated.

While developing this rich culture was important to the whole company, I was surprised to find how much the social committee members themselves benefited. Here are some benefits that I observed.

1. They were able to use their natural talents, and people are happiest when they are able to use their God-given gifts.

2. They were recognized in a public way for their service.

3. They had ongoing input into our culture, which gave them a sense of ownership. The committee members were usually manager level and below, people who might not be able to impact culture otherwise.

MULTIPLE LOCATIONS

If your company has offices in multiple locations, each location should have a social committee and its own budget. You could assign certain things that need to be celebrated by each group, and their efforts should always be aligned with the goals and values of the company. However, each area has unique events and customs, and it will be more effective to allow each group to have events that will mean the most to them.

NON-OFFICE EMPLOYEES

Creating social events for non-office employees is a bit trickier. If someone works off-site, but in the same area as a company office, he or she should be invited to the office events. For sales and other groups who are disbursed across the country or world, they generally have annual and/or quarterly meetings that they attend in person. At these meetings, I recommend that you create opportunities for them to socialize and celebrate accomplishments.

Also, you could recognize special events in an employee's life (e.g., birthday, birth of child, work anniversary, death of a loved one) with a gift delivered to his or her home. There are actually companies who will manage this for you. You give them the employee's information and they handle the rest. Sending a gift to a non-office employee helps assure them that they are not forgotten and makes them feel like a part of the company.

MAGNETIC EMPLOYEE PROGRAMS

Create and implement
a powerful rewards strategy

CHAPTER 14

Maximize Your Return on Investment (ROI)

THE COST OF EMPLOYEE PROGRAMS (e.g., compensation, benefits) is generally the largest expense for companies. We also know that this is a necessary expense, and employee programs must be done right to attract, retain, and engage employees. *Given the expense, rewards, and risks, shouldn't there be a strategy around employee programs to ensure money is spent in the right places and that the returns on that money are maximized?*

Magnetic Employee Programs are designed strategically to attract, retain and engage employees. These programs maximize a company's return on investment (ROI), and include the financial as well as the non-financial rewards of work. Magnetic Employee Programs take into account what employees really desire. These programs are managed holistically, not piecemeal, and are constantly assessed for effectiveness.

The most powerful strategy that I've found to create Magnetic Employee Programs is **Total Rewards**.

EMERGENCE OF TOTAL REWARDS

Companies started realizing the need for a comprehensive approach to employee programs in the 1990s, and the concept of Total Rewards emerged. It was designed as a new way to look at compensation and benefits, and make programs more effective by bringing the human element to the forefront with a focus on the non-financial rewards of work (e.g., work-life programs, employee development, recognition). Total Rewards gives the non-financial rewards a seat at the strategy table.

In the 1990s, the demographics of the workforce were changing as well. More women were joining the workforce, and the demand for more flexibility and better work-life programs was on the rise. I feel like women in the Baby Boomer generation broke through the glass ceiling, and my generation (Gen X) stepped in and decided to get comfortable. Coupled with technology, the demands for more work-life balance programs started to be recognized in the 2000s as a human resources priority to recruit and retain high-caliber employees.

> I feel like women in the Baby Boomer generation broke through the glass ceiling, and my generation (Gen X) stepped in and decided to get comfortable.

When the millennials came on the scene, there was an increased demand for work-life balance from both men and women. This generation is not as focused on money as much as previous generations. They place a high value on programs like career development and a good work environment. They demand the whole package! Millennials want to have fulfilling careers AND happy lives.

The Total Rewards strategy is designed to effectively manage the everchanging workforce and achieve the objectives of the company.

CHAPTER 15

Total Rewards Strategy

WHILE CULTURE IS THE HEART of a company, a Total Rewards program is the hands and feet. Establishing a Total Rewards strategy helps to ensure that employee programs become a strategic driving force in the accomplishment of organizational goals.

Total Rewards includes everything that an employee values in an employment deal. Total Reward elements are typically slotted into the following six categories:

- Compensation

- Benefits

- Work-Life Programs

- Recognition

- Performance Management

- Talent Development

Creating a company's Total Rewards strategy is the art of combining these six elements into a package that is unique to your company. It should build synergy between individual programs, ensure that money is being spent in the right places, and improve the *perceived* value of programs through communications.

We implemented a Total Rewards strategy at Scandipharm in part to reduce turnover; also, because it simply made good business sense. I have a finance degree, and I think in terms of ROI (Return on Investment). When I read about Total Rewards, I could see that it was a better way to maximize ROI on the large amount of money that we spent on employee programs. I also believed that it would improve our ability to attract top talent and reduce the costs of turnover, and it did!

The success of any company is determined in large part by what they do with their resources. Frequently, companies implement various programs over time to meet employee needs. However, taking a bird's-eye view of all of the employee programs and constantly assessing them as a whole is more effective. This assessment involves ensuring that the Total Rewards program is aligned with the company's business objectives and culture.

The Total Rewards assessment also takes into account external influences such as economics, labor markets, cultural norms, and regulatory environments that impact the current and potential workforce. To get ahead of the competition, the Total Rewards strategy should be designed to overcome the external challenges and outshine competition for top talent. **Instead of being reactive (why are we suddenly losing our employees?), it is being proactive (understand the shifting needs of the workforce and adjusting programs as needed to retain employees).**

Total Rewards is sometimes referred to as the "employment deal" or the "employment value proposition (EVP)." In the *2014 Global Talent Management and Rewards Study* by Towers Watson, companies with highly-evolved employment deals significantly outperformed organizations that did not have a stated employment deal.

EMPLOYMENT DEAL GROUPS	FINANCIAL PERFORMANCE	SUSTAINABLE ENGAGEMENT	FINANCIAL PERFORMANCE	SUSTAINABLE ENGAGEMENT
Highly evolved*	25.9%	20%	20.1%	24.8%
Tactical**	15.5%	6.9%	13.0%	7.4%
Ratio of highly evolved to tactical	1.7	2.9	1.5	3.3

* Organizations with a formally articulated, well-executed employment deal that is customized for different employee segments and differentiated from their competitors

** Organizations without a formally articulated employment deal and accompanying Total Rewards strategy

Highly-evolved employment deals significantly outperformed organizations that did not have a stated employment deal.

This study shows the benefits of having a Total Rewards strategy. In the next section, you will learn how to build that strategy.

CHAPTER 16

How to Build a
Total Rewards Strategy

THE GOOD NEWS IS THAT creating a Total Rewards program doesn't have to cost any money. It is a strategy. It is all about making more with what you've got. When you identify holes in your programs, you will probably want to shore those up, which may or may not cost you money. How much you spend is really up to you. As an added bonus, you may find programs that aren't relevant anymore, and you can discard them.

The procedure for creating a Total Rewards program is provided below.

STEP 1: ASSESS CURRENT PROGRAMS

Make an Inventory List

Building a Total Rewards strategy starts by making an inventory list of all of your current employee programs – financial and non-financial. Group them by Total Rewards category (Compensation, Benefits, Work-Life, Recognition, Performance, and Talent Development). I have provided lists of common programs in the following sections.

I recommend building the inventory list in chart form so that you can make notes and add other columns (e.g., annual costs, vendor) on each program as needed. A chart will also allow you to easily add rows for new or desired programs. A basic inventory list is provided below as an example.

PROGRAMS	NOTES
Compensation	
Base Pay	
Short-term Incentive	
Long-term Incentive	
Benefits	
Healthcare Program	
Short-term Disability	
Long-term Disability	
Work-Life Programs	
Paid Time Off (PTO)	
Telework Program	
Flexible Spending Account	
Recognition	
Length of Service Awards	
Employee of the Quarter	
President's Award	
Performance Management	
Goal Establishment Process	
Mid-year Review	
Assessment and Reward Process	
Talent Development	
On-Boarding Process	
Manager Training Program	
Training Resource Guide	

Example of a Total Rewards inventory list

If you have employees in different countries, the programs are probably very different, so it may be easier to have separate inventory lists for each country.

TIP: This is a great tool to have on hand in the event of a merger/

acquisition. I've been through a lot of these, and I can tell you that it makes the due diligence process easier by having a prepared inventory list of programs. Also, it helps to facilitate the integration of employee programs across companies because it provides a basis for comparison.

I've provided a worksheet on my website (paschakelley.com) that will assist you with creating your inventory list and assessment of each program.

Assess Internal Environment

The Total Rewards strategy should drive accomplishment of business goals and help create a Magnetic Culture. In order to do this, the inventory list should be assessed to determine if the programs are aligned with the company's vision, mission, goals, and culture.

In order to determine if your current programs are providing engagement, you should ask your employees directly. Get feedback from your employees on what is important to them and how they see your current programs. This is frequently done via a survey. There are several online survey providers that are inexpensive.

Exit interviews are another way to find out how effective your employee programs are. Ask if there is something in the employee programs or work experience that you could have changed that would have made them want to stay. Hint: If you're having a lot of exit interviews, you might need to change some things.

Creating an Employee Advisory Group (EAG) is another great way to get employees' points of view on an ongoing basis. At Scandipharm, we had a group called the Total Rewards Network, comprised of a mix of people from different levels and departments. They met once a quarter and provided HR with insight on the pulse of the workforce.

Examples of topics to discuss with an EAG follow.

- Are a lot of employees considering leaving? If so, why? Can we do anything about it?

- How are we doing on communicating our programs? Do employees understand what they have? If no, how can we improve communications?

- What do employees value about our company? What keeps them here? How can we expand on that?

- We are considering adding/changing an employee program. How do you think that will be received by the employees?

The members of the EAG can also serve as ambassadors for new or changing programs. If you give them information before other employees, it makes them feel important (an insider), and they are more likely to champion the changes with other employees.

When selecting EAG members, you should choose people who are able to maintain confidences, are not gossips, would not try to use it for political or personal gain, and have a level head on their shoulders.

Assess External Influences

Your Total Rewards strategy needs to take into account the ever-changing external environment, which includes government regulations, attitudes of the work force, labor supply, etc. You need to understand the unique influences in the marketplace and build a strategy that will attract, retain, and engage employees in that environment.

You can get information on the external marketplace from professional associations, business journals, and consultants. However you get your information, don't stop at this one assessment. The workforce is changing at lightning speed, so this assessment should be constant. Some current examples of trends in the external marketplace include:

1. Baby Boomers retiring

2. Shortage of skilled workers

3. More woman in the work place

4. Flexibility is now expected instead of requested

5. Millennials are the largest group in the workplace

Millennials place a high value on non-financial rewards such as flexibility, work environment, time for community service, etc. This is actually good news for business leaders who get it. By this I mean they are willing to ditch old-school ways of doing things and are open to new ways of working. I've seen leaders who won't budge on working in new ways, no matter how much research data is put before them.

For business leaders who are willing to advance in the way they do business, this is a great way to get ahead of the competition. Charles Darwin said, "It is not the strongest of the species that survives, nor the most intelligent that survives. It is the one that is most adaptable to change."

STEP 2: DEVELOP THE TOTAL REWARDS STRATEGY

Taking into account all of the research that you did in Step 1, you can now develop your Total Rewards strategy. First, consider the following:

- **Strengths** – What is working? Determine what makes your company unique. How can you use this to differentiate your company from others?

- **Risks** – Are your employees about to abandon ship? What can you do to entice them to stay?

- **Zombies** – At Ziglar, we call employees who are **not** engaged "Zombies." Our goal is to help companies turn their Zombies into productive people. Do you have a Zombie problem in your company? How can you bring them to life?

Now, go back to your Total Rewards inventory list and make notes about the individual programs, what is working, and what is not. Make suggestions for changes where needed. This could include modifying existing programs to respond to employee and potential employee needs. This could include eliminating or phasing out programs that are not providing value or are not cost effective.

Next, make a list of any programs you want to add. You probably will not be able to make changes to programs all at once. Therefore, I suggest that you prioritize changes based on critical need and budget.

Finally, sell your new Total Rewards strategy and the changes that you are requesting to the powers that be. Gain approval and implement!

Consider setting up measurements to track the impact of your Total Rewards strategy. Some examples include turnover metrics and employee engagement surveys.

STEP 3: CREATE A COMMUNICATION PLAN

To be effective, your Total Rewards program must have a communication strategy. A Total Rewards program without a communication strategy is like a car without wheels. You can sit in it, but it won't get you anywhere! The Total Rewards package and individual components should be communicated frequently with employees. The communication strategy should provide a picture of the rich program the company offers, and ensure that every employee knows how to take full advantage of all that is offered.

When we built our Total Rewards program, I found that there were benefits I didn't even know about! For example, I found out that our healthcare provider offered a wellness website for free, and very few people knew about it. By communicating this wellness program to employees as part of our Total Rewards program, we increased the *perceived* value of our benefits program without spending a dime!

Total Rewards communication is so important that it has its own chapter, so I won't get into the details here.

STEP 4: EVALUATE AND REVISE

External and internal environments are constantly changing. Therefore, to be effective, you should consistently assess your Total Rewards program and make changes as necessary. Try to stay ahead of the curve, not behind it.

I find that it is helpful to schedule this assessment to occur right before the annual budget process. This way, if you need to ask for additional funding for programs, you are prepared to fight the battle for money. Also, if you tie your annual assessment to another business process, it helps ensure that it gets done.

To create and maintain competitive advantage, your Total Rewards strategy cannot be stagnant. It should be a constant process of assessment and improvement.

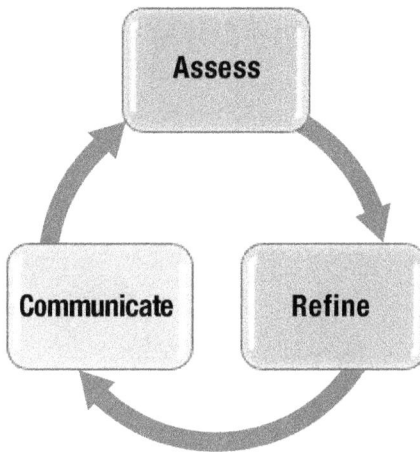

Total Rewards assessment and improvement process

In the next sections, I provide an overview of each component of the Total Rewards toolkit.

CHAPTER 17

Compensation

COMPENSATION IS THE BEST-KNOWN COMPONENT of the Total Rewards family. It is also the most complex and expensive component. Since I'm a numbers gal, I love working in compensation. There is a lot that I would like to share about compensation strategy, but I'm going to refrain from geeking out and just give you some basics and tips.

Compensation is divided into two categories: fixed compensation and variable compensation

1. **Fixed compensation** is also known as "base pay." This is an annual amount or rate that is fixed and is not based on performance. Base pay includes:

   a. **Salary** – compensation paid on a weekly, biweekly, or monthly basis

   b. **Hourly Rate** – compensation paid by the hours worked

   c. **Piece Work** – payment is based on the rate of production

2. **Variable compensation** is based on the results achieved by the individual and/or the company. It is also called "pay at risk" or "incentive compensation." Variable compensation can be paid on a short-term (one year or less) basis or long-term (greater than one year) basis. The time of payout depends on the performance goals that it is tied to.

    a. **Short-term incentive (STI)** – The payments are generally made on a quarterly or annual basis. They include bonus, commissions, and profit-sharing plans.

    b. **Long-term incentives (LTI)** – This pays out sometime in the future based on achievement by the company and/or individual (trigger event). It is designed to retain employees long-term because they do not receive full payment if they leave before the trigger event occurs. LTI is generally stock-based and includes stock options, stock appreciation rights (SARs), restricted stock/restricted stock units (RSUs), and other long-term performance awards.

The combination of fixed and variable pay is called the **Total Compensation** package. When you benchmark your compensation to other companies, you should look at the Total Compensation package instead of just base pay. Companies at different stages of development (e.g., start-up, growth, mature) have different mixes of these pay elements. For example, start-up companies usually have a greater percentage of variable compensation, so if the company wins, the employees win, and vice versa.

ADMINISTRATION

Pay practices should be communicated effectively to employees, and managers should be well-trained on their role in administering compensation. The level of detail shared with employees on compensation programs varies widely across companies. **Even if you don't provide detailed numbers (e.g., salary ranges, hourly rate scale) to employees, at least communicate the how, why, and when of your pay practices.** Employees will feel uncertain if it appears that compensation is a deep, dark secret that leaders do not talk about. I can guarantee you that employees talk and will make up their own theories if none is provided by the company.

PAY INCREASES

I recommend that compensation decisions be aligned with performance. Even though base pay does not vary in amount paid based on performance, you can tie *increases* to performance. Let's face it, you only have a certain amount of money that you can give to employees. Don't you want to give your high performers the bulk of it? To align base pay decisions with performance, you should plan to make pay raise decisions following your performance review cycle.

HANDLING COMPLAINERS

It will save you a lot of time and headaches if you have only one time a year that pay raises are considered, and employees know that the decisions are tied to their performance. There are always those employees who have a friend working at another company in the same job making more than they do. Or, they have done their own market research (usually on Salary.com) and think that they should be paid more – right now!

When you have one of these people show up in your office, you can simply explain that pay raises are given one time a year. At this time, **total compensation** is compared to the market, and internal equity is also reviewed. You can further explain that paying employees fairly is a business priority, and it takes time to make good pay decisions. Also, raises are contingent on performance scores.

At this point, the employee should walk out reasonably satisfied. If the employee does not, you probably have an issue on your hands. If you did give this employee a raise, he would most likely come back and demand another raise soon. These kinds of people usually do not fit in a Magnetic Culture, and you will probably have to show them the door eventually.

PROMOTIONS

I recommend that promotions be made at a certain time of year as well. It works best if you do this at the same time you are reviewing salary increases. Handling complainers works the same way it does with salary increases. Simply explain the process.

Now, there are some exceptions to this rule, such as a higher-level position becoming available and an employee filling that position. Also, in an extreme case where an employee leaves or a job is eliminated, and another employee absorbs the work responsibility in addition to doing his or her own job. This could be a person that you consider promoting sooner. However, I do not recommend that you give the promotion immediately. Give the person time to see if he or she can manage both jobs successfully. Many times the burden is too great, and the employee can't manage it. You don't want to give a promotion prematurely as you can't or shouldn't take it back. However, I recommend that you use rewards and recognition in the short-term to show the employee appreciation for their extra work.

Giving promotions to well-deserving employees was the most joyful part of my job. It was also one of the most difficult because I didn't give promotions to everyone who requested one. I always strived to be very fair. I assessed each promotion request carefully, and looked across the organization for employees who did not request a promotion but deserved one. I had to be firm with those who tried to sway me in the wrong direction. I was not always liked for my decisions, and I have the battle scars to prove it!

The bottom line is that the promotion process has to be fair across the entire company. When you give a promotion to someone, you are making a statement about their work and their behavior to the rest of the company.

If you give a promotion to someone who does not deserve it from a work-level stand point, performance or a behavior stand point, you will be stirring up more problems for yourself. Fixing one problem can cause many more problems to rise. Other employees take note of who is promoted. If they feel that they are doing the same level of work as the person promoted, they will probably request a promotion as well. Also, if a person of poor character is promoted, employees will think that this is acceptable behavior and many will follow suit or be disenfranchised.

I encourage you to give promotions to those who deserve them based on work, performance and behavior. Keep in mind that promotions are one of the greatest forms of reward and recognition, and you will get more of what you reward.

COMPENSATION STATEMENTS

Making your compensation decisions on an annual cycle aligned with performance also makes communications more efficient and effective. I recommend sending out a comprehensive annual Compensation Statement to employees following the annual compensation decision process.

An annual compensation statement should begin with a brief letter from the president or other leader on company results for the year and a summary of major accomplishments. This is particularly important if compensation decisions are based on company achievements. The letter should also thank the employees for their contributions.

What the Compensation Statement covers depends on the types of decisions made annually. The statement could include:

- Individual performance rating score
- Pay increases

- Short-term incentive payouts

- Long-term incentive awards and payouts

- Promotions and impact on pay and benefits

- Effective dates for pay increases and promotions, and when payments will be made

It is helpful to provide as much detail as possible. Provided below is an example of a compensation statement.

Compensation Statement

BASE SALARY ADJUSTMENT FOR 2019		
2018 Salary		$50,000
Increase	4%	$2,000
2019 Salary		**$52,000**
The new salary will be effective January 1, 2019.		
BONUS PAYMENT FOR 2018		
Corporate Performance Factor	5%	$2,500
Individual Performance Factor	10%	$5,000
Total Bonus		**$7,500**
Bonus is calculated as your 2018 Salary multiplied by each factor. Payment will be made to your account on December 5, 2018.		
STOCK OPTION AWARD		
Number		10.000
Date Granted		10/1/18
Grant Price		$7
Award Agreement attached. Please sign and return to HR.		

Comprehensive statements help increase the perceived value of compensation. **Communicating the whole, instead of individual pieces at various times, helps employees appreciate their total package.** This is particularly important if an employee is unhappy with one part of his or her compensation. Understanding the total compensation package could retain this employee.

Compensation is an emotional area for employees. Having their compensation explained clearly helps dial down the anxiety. Knowing that they will receive this information at the same time each year gives employees a degree of security.

A compensation statement that communicates clearly and has an appealing look is like wrapping paper. You are giving employees a good compensation package. By wrapping it in nice paper with a bow on top (Compensation Statement), you improve the perceived value of the gift.

CHAPTER 18

Benefits

BENEFITS INCLUDE A WIDE VARIETY of health, income protection (short-term and long-term disability), and savings and retirement programs. In general, benefits are designed to provide security for employees and their families. Below is a list of the most common benefits programs:

Health and Wellness Programs

- Medical healthcare plan
- Dental healthcare plan
- Prescription drug plan
- Vision plan
- Telemedicine services
- Life insurance/ Accidental Death & Dismemberment (AD&D)
- Short-term disability (STD) insurance
- Long-term disability (LTD) insurance
- Health savings accounts (HSA)
- Flexible spending accounts (FSA)

- Health reimbursement accounts (HRAs)
- Employee assistance programs (EAP)
- Immunization clinics or promotions
- Wellness programs and wellness incentives (e.g., cash and non-cash prizes, recognition, awards)
- Health-risk assessment (HRA)
- Health advocacy programs
- Health coaching
- 24-hour nurse line
- Use of wearable technology for encouraging wellness results
- On-site medical clinic or nurse
- Seminars, webinars, or literature to promote wellness and well-being
- Stress-reduction programs/offerings (e.g., yoga, massage, meditation)
- Tobacco-smoking cessation support
- Nutrition counseling (on-site or covered by medical plan)
- Weight-management programs
- Subsidized weight-loss programs
- Discounted fitness club membership/fitness-related subsidies
- On-site fitness center and fitness classes
- Healthy cafeteria options and vending machine options

Retirement

- Defined benefit plan
- Defined contribution plan (e.g., 401(k), 403(b), 457 plans)
- Non-qualified deferred compensation plan

- Retiree healthcare benefits
- Employee stock ownership plan (ESOP)

Other Benefits and Perks

- Employee stock purchase plan (ESPP)
- Long-term care insurance
- Auto/home insurance
- Pet insurance
- Legal insurance, referral or consultation
- Identify theft insurance
- Concierge services
- Free parking or parking subsidy
- Commuter/transportation benefits or subsidy
- Company car or car allowance
- Cell phone (employer-issued, monthly allowance or reimbursement)
- Laptop computer
- Student loan debt repayment assistance
- Debt management (e.g., counseling, education)
- Personal financial-planning services (e.g., seminars, access to financial planners, estate planning)
- Personal tax services

As you can see, there are many benefits programs to choose from at different price points.

DIG FOR GOLD!

Make sure that you are maximizing everything that you already have from your existing benefit providers. **Ask if they offer any additional programs for FREE**. For example, life insurance companies frequently offer an employee assistance program (EAP) for free to their customers. In this case, the EAP should be part of your Total Rewards program and communicated to employees.

Once you get all of the free stuff, find out if there are benefit programs they offer as an **add-on at a low cost**. You might find they offer a program that your employees have been requesting.

Also, ask benefit providers if they will provide **education to your employees** to enhance the perceived value of their programs, and help your employees receive greater benefit from their programs. By doing this, you are increasing your value/cost ratio of existing programs.

There are a lot of benefit providers out there competing for business. When you are comparing programs, make sure that you assess the full range of services that they provide and that they are willing to educate your employees on their services. Benefits are expensive. Select providers who will help you get the most bang for your buck!

CHAPTER 19

Work-Life Programs

WORK-LIFE BALANCE IS MY PASSION because I love my family and I love to work. Sadly, my domestic skills are minimal. I am perfectly happy in my office, but if you put me in a kitchen, I get grumpy really fast! So, being able to work and care for my family has always been important to me. Personally, I'm thankful that work-life programs have risen to the forefront as a business issue.

Work-Life programs are those that help employees achieve success in their personal lives as well as in business. The most common work-life programs are provided below:

Time Off

- Paid Time Off (PTO) (e.g., vacation, sick leave, personal leave)

- Holiday pay and floating holidays

- Bereavement leave

- Paid sabbaticals

- Paid parental leave

- Paid caregiver leave

- Unpaid, job-protected time off (beyond legal requirements)

Caring for Dependents

- Childcare resources and referral services
- Eldercare resources and referral services
- Childcare Center – On-site, nearby, subsidies, or discounts
- Backup childcare or eldercare
- Dependent care spending accounts
- Travel-related dependent care expense reimbursement
- Support for employees with special-needs children
- Lactation-support services
- Adoption assistance or reimbursement
- College preparation planning and savings plans (529 plans)
- Employee scholarship/ student aide/ loans

Workplace Flexibility

- Flex time (ability to adjust workday start and end times)
- Telework
- Compressed workweek
- Part-time/reduced work schedules
- Shift flexibility
- Alternative worksites
- Hoteling
- Annualized hours
- Job sharing
- Phased return to work after leave of absence
- Phased retirement
- Career on- and off-ramps

- Seasonal scheduling (e.g., summer hours)
- Results-based work environment

As you can see, there are numerous ways to provide work-life balance to your employees. Keep in mind that these programs are investments in your bottom line. Work-life balance is critically important to your employees, and they will jump ship to another company who provides a better overall life for them.

Work-life programs are a key part of recruiting top talent. People are no longer working for just a paycheck. They are working towards a dream – their dream. Companies who help their employees achieve their dreams win their hearts.

ZIGLAR WHEEL OF LIFE

I can't talk about work-life balance without talking about the Ziglar Wheel of Life. At Ziglar, not only have I found work-life balance, I have the pleasure of teaching it to other people and making their lives better! You see, true success is not found only in your career, but in your whole life.

Ziglar Wheel of Life©

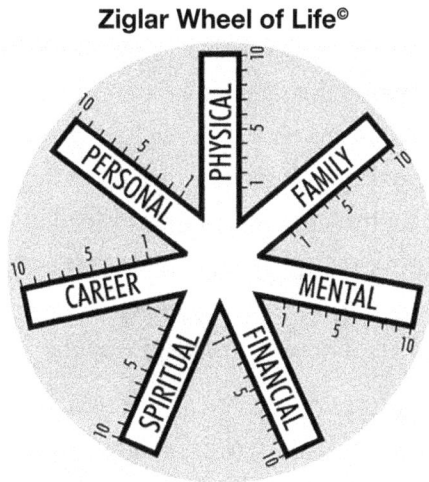

The Ziglar philosophy is to help people live balanced and fulfilled lives. Each spoke of the wheel represents an area of life: Physical,

Family, Mental, Financial, Spiritual, Career, and Personal. All of these spokes are intertwined; they impact one another. So, you can't just be strong in one or two and truly have a balanced life.

It is amazing to me that Zig came up with this before work-life balance was a thing. This model is what employees want. They want to have whole lives and be successful in all areas. Companies who understand this—really understand it—will create competitive advantage.

On the Wheel of Life, there are tick marks from 1-10. This is related to the assessment of each area. I've provided an easy-to-use Ziglar assessment worksheet on my website that will help you determine where you are on each spoke of the wheel.

After you determine your score for each spoke of the wheel, plot the numbers and connect them. Ideally, you will have a circle, which means that you are developing equally in each area. If you have an area that is flat (lower score than other areas), you know that you are not giving it enough attention and need to strengthen that area.

For me, the Ziglar Wheel of Life is a visual that reminds me of all the things that are important in my life. I'm very task oriented, and the Ziglar Wheel of Life helps me remember to work in the softer areas like building relationships with friends and family.

When I feel that I'm falling down in one area, I'll place more attention on strengthening that area. For example, sometimes I feel that my spending is out of control. To get me back in control, I'll listen to a Dave Ramsey podcast for thirty minutes to an hour each day. Pretty soon I find myself squirreling away money instead of spending it. Once I'm back in control of my finances, I'll let up on educating myself in this area, because there is always another area that needs work. As Christy Wright says in her book *Business Boutique*,

---

Life balance isn't about doing everything in your life for an equal amount of time. It's about doing the right things at the right time.

(WRIGHT, 2017)

CHAPTER 20

Recognition Programs

RECOGNITION IS A SHARP TOOL in the Total Rewards toolkit. Dale Carnegie said, "People work for money but go the extra mile for recognition, praise, and rewards." (Johnson, 2016)

In a ten-year global study by HealthStream Research and O.C. Tanner, they found a link between recognition and financial performance. Employee recognition impacts Operating Margin in a significant way. (Operating Margin is a ratio of operating income to sales.) According to the data, **companies with the highest quartile of recognition of excellence report an Operating Margin of 6.6%, while those in the lowest quartile report 1.7%.**

Recognition comes in two forms – formal and informal.

FORMAL RECOGNITION

In this section, I'll talk about the *formal* recognition programs that are part of a Total Rewards program. These are the award programs that have defined criteria for receiving the awards. Formal recognition programs provide the infrastructure to make sure that recognition happens, and that the right behaviors and actions are rewarded.

According to WorldatWork's *Trends in Employee Recognition* report (May 2017), the most common recognition programs are as follows:

- Length of service
- Above and beyond performance
- Programs to motivate specific behaviors
- Peer to peer
- Retirement
- Programs that improve biometric indices through wellness initiatives
- Sales performance
- Suggestions/ideas
- Safety performance
- Employee of the year, month, etc.
- Major family event (e.g., birth, wedding)
- Attendance

HOW TO DEVELOP AN EFFECTIVE PROGRAM

To create a recognition program, you need to decide first what behaviors and actions you want to drive with your program. In the WorldatWork's *Trends in Employee Recognition* report (May 2017), the following are the objectives/ goals of the participants' recognition programs.

	2013	2015	2017
n=	374	376	282
Recognize years of service	77%	79%	79%
Create/maintain a positive work environment	74%	77%	77%
Create/maintain a culture of recognition	73%	75%	76%
Motivate high performance	72%	72%	71%
Reinforce desired behaviors	66%	65%	69%
Support organizational mission/values	56%	60%	64%
Increase morale	60%	62%	59%
Support becoming/remaining an employer of choice	37%	40%	44%
Increase retention or decrease turnover	41%	51%	42%
Encourage loyalty	43%	41%	38%
Support a culture of change	18%	24%	25%
Provide line of sight to company goals	24%	27%	24%
Encourage safe practices	n/a	22%	23%
Other	5%	2%	1%

Objectives/goals of recognition programs

As you can see, there are a lot of uses for recognition programs, and most center on enhancing culture, retention, motivation, and engagement. This is a great place to load up your Total Rewards toolbox to create competitive advantage.

The most effective recognition programs offer several different ways to recognize people. Provided below are the four main categories for recognition programs.

1. Career Recognition

These awards are the foundation of formal recognition programs as they have been around for the longest period of time. They include length-of-service awards and retirement awards. Typically, these awards involve public recognition and some type of gift or trophy.

- **Length-of-Service** awards honor people on the anniversary of their hire date. They are usually celebrated on the one-year anniversary and every five-year increment after that (5-year,

10-year, 15-year, etc.). The main purpose of this award is to promote retention.

- **Retirement** awards are a respectful way to say goodbye to an employee. Above all, it is simply the right thing to do. From a practical standpoint, retiring employees will tell others in the community, and possibly online, how they were treated as they departed the company. Also, retirement awards and the public recognition that accompanies them, say volumes to employees who remain. If Old Bob is tossed out the door un-ceremoniously, it tells other employees that they will be treated the same way, which decreases engagement. Of course, the opposite is true when employees are honored and treated well upon retirement.

2. Above-and-Beyond Performance

These awards are given for significant achievements that exceed expec-tations. The recognition is typically public and involves a certificate, plaque, or trophy. There is frequently a monetary award or gift/prize as well. Employee of the Month, Quarter, Year are examples of these types of awards.

Above-and-Beyond awards should be aligned with company goals and Core Values. The award should only be given to people who have a significant accomplishment and faithfully demonstrate the company's values. Don't award the bull in the china shop who exceeds expecta-tions on a project but takes other people down in the process. What gets rewarded gets repeated. If you award this type of behavior, others will follow, and good people will leave the company.

3. Programs to Motivate Specific Behaviors

Recognition is a great way to motivate certain behaviors and actions. Provided below is a list of some of the most common target behaviors in this category.

- Demonstrate Core Values

- Achieve sales goals

- Provide excellent customer service

- Refer people to the company (referral program)

- Improve health (wellness initiatives)

- Give suggestions/ideas

- No injuries (safety awards)

- Attend work (attendance awards)

The design of the program is unique for each type of award.

4. On-The-Spot Awards

These awards are also called ad hoc, ongoing, and day-to-day recognition. They award smaller accomplishments such as extra effort, a good idea, working extra hours, good attitude in a difficult situation, etc. In *The Carrot Principle*, it is recommended that on-the-spot awards be

- Frequent

- Specific

- Timely

In a formal recognition program, the company provides managers with tools for on-the-spot awards, and the knowledge of how and when to give the awards. Some examples of these tools include thank-you notes and gift certificates/ cards.

INFORMAL RECOGNITION

On-The-Spot Awards also fall into the *informal* recognition category. Informal recognition includes pats on the back, thanking people (in person, via email or handwritten note), praising them in front of a group of people, etc.

Informal recognition is just as important as formal recognition, maybe more so, but there is no formal structure to make sure it happens. Sam Walton said, "Appreciate everything your associates do for the business. Nothing else can quite substitute for a few well-chosen, well-timed, sincere words of praise. They're absolutely free and worth a fortune." (Windust, 2015)

In a study by OfficeTeam and the International Association of Administrative Professionals (IAAP), administrative professionals ranked an in-person thank you and the boss sharing accomplishment with senior management as their #1 most valued form of recognition. However, managers ranked job promotion and cash as the two most valued forms of recognition.

What the administrative professionals actually wanted was FREE to the company! For leaders who understand the power of informal recognition, they can save money while creating engagement.

What can you do to ensure informal recognition is happening in your company? First, make sure you are setting the example. **People will follow what you do more than what you say**. Second, ensure that you have good manager training on recognition, and tie your managers' effectiveness to their performance scores.

CHAPTER 21

Performance Management

I CAN HEAR THE GROANS now. Most people hate to talk about performance management. Let's face it – most employees don't like getting performance reviews, and most managers don't like giving them. I think this is because most companies are simply doing it wrong. They do not provide the right tools and training to managers, and performance discussions only take place once a year. (I'll discuss how to improve this later in this chapter.)

I think of performance management programs as the *connector* piece in the Total Rewards toolbox. It connects company goals and values to individual employees. Performance management is a system to help employees know what is expected of them and how their work contributes to the company's goals. People need to feel that they are making an impact on the company, and a performance management program gives them that line of sight. David Lapin said, "Money can motivate people, but it takes a strong, well-defined purpose to truly inspire greatness."

An effective performance management program defines expected behaviors and serves as a manager tool to discuss behavior with employees. It also facilitates employee development and coaching conversations.

Performance management then connects employee performance and behavior to compensation, recognition, and talent development. It also makes some work-life programs (e.g., flexible work schedules) possible because people are measured on what they accomplish and do not have to be seen doing it.

COMPANY GOALS AND CORE VALUES	⮕	PERFORMANCE MANAGEMENT	⮕	EMPLOYEE REWARDS
• Vision • Mission • Goals • Core Values		• Set employee goals • Measure accomplishments • Assess behaviors • Determine training needed		• Compensation • Recognition • Talent development

Performance Management connects the achievement of company goals and Core Value to Employee Rewards.

HOW TO IMPROVE PERFORMANCE MANAGEMENT

With the workforce changing at dizzying speeds, the way we manage employee performance needs to change as well. According to an article written by Gallup, *3 Reasons Why Performance Development Wins in the Workplace*, "Employees used to expect to work for a boss. Now, they're looking for a coach." The article reports that employees want the following from their managers:

- Job clarity and priorities
- Ongoing feedback and communication
- Opportunities to learn and grow
- Accountability

According to Gallup's analysis of high-performing teams, performance reviews can improve effectiveness by being *achievement-oriented*, *fair*, *accurate*, and *developmental*.

Achievement-Oriented

I have yet to find a man, however exalted his station, who did not do better work and put forth greater effort under a spirit of approval than under a spirit of criticism.

— CHARLES SCHWAB (WINDUST, 2015)

Performance reviews should first emphasize what the employee did right. I think this is where performance reviews get a bad rap. People are afraid of the negative things that their managers are going to say. If a manager tells them what they did right first, it makes the negative feedback easier to take. Coach Bud Grant said, "If you have something critical to say to a player, preface it by saying something positive. That way when you get to the criticism, at least you know he'll be listening." (Roskvist, 2017)

When giving correction, managers should describe what good performance and behavior looks like. Make sure they understand the expectations. Then, discuss specific ways they can improve. Performance reviews should be about continual development, and employees should not be surprised by what they hear at year end. If an employee is not performing or behaving as expected, they should be coached on a regular basis (daily or weekly) – not just at year end.

Finally, end on a positive note. Point out the employees' strengths and what they are capable of accomplishing. Encourage employees to take ownership of their development, and let them know that they are valued.

This positive–negative–positive approach sandwiches the negative comments so that they are more palatable.

The positive-negative-positive approach to giving corrections

121

Fair and Accurate

Over a year, business priorities and individual responsibilities can change. If a performance review is only done once a year, it is likely that the goals set at the beginning of the year need to be adjusted. For example, an employee takes on an urgent new project during the year, which results in another goal not being achieved due to the extra time required by the new project. *Should the employee be penalized for not accomplishing a goal because he has taken on more work?* No! I can tell you that this has happened to me, and it was demoralizing. There is no incentive to take on more work if employees are only going to be penalized for it.

> **When employees are involved in their goal setting, they are 4x more likely to be engaged than other employees.**
>
> — GALLUP

This is why managers should meet with employees to readjust performance expectations any time there is a change in responsibilities. Both parties need to be clear about how new responsibilities affect the year-end performance assessment. At minimum, managers need to meet with employees every six months to review performance expectations and provide any coarse corrections.

Another way to make performance reviews more fair and accurate is to involve the employee in setting his or her goals. Gallup reports that when employees are involved in their goal setting, they are four times more likely to be engaged than other employees.

Developmental

Development is one of the top wants of employees. The performance review process is an excellent way to provide that development. By incorporating an employee development section into your performance management program, you can help ensure that development conversations are taking place between managers and employees.

Performance management doesn't have to be a dreaded task.

Performance management should emphasize achievement, resolve employee problems, and develop employees to be their personal best. If done right, performance management can improve employees' performance while boosting engagement and retention.

CHAPTER 22

Talent Development

IN A GALLUP BLOG POST entitled "37 Workplaces That Stand Out From the Rest," the authors state that the best companies "have an intense and intentional focus on engaging their employees" (Harter, 2017). In this article, they give six ways these companies achieve engagement. You will notice that several involve employee development, and manager training or skills that should be taught in manager training (e.g., engaging employees, communication, accountability).

- Employee engagement is a business priority; it is part of their strategy to achieve competitive advantage.
- Leaders communicate openly and effectively.
- They provide excellent leadership and management training.
- Managers are held accountable for the engagement of their team as well as their team's overall performance.
- Individual employee training is a priority.
- They give their employees what they need to be successful at their jobs: clear work expectations, tools to do the job, training, and facilitation of positive coworker relationships.

Benjamin Franklin said, "An investment in knowledge always pays the best interest." (Franklin, 2011) I think this is why talent development is one of the most sought-after tools in the Total Rewards toolkit. It includes programs that provide the opportunities to improve employees' skills and behaviors.

Employee development starts with the onboarding process for new employees and should take place continuously thereafter. To ensure that talent development takes place, the company should provide a set of processes, programs, and resources for employees, including:

- Onboarding process
- Performance management program
- Manager training
- On-site training
- Budget specifically for training and development

I also recommend creating a Training Resource Guide that provides managers and employees with a list of training opportunities and ideas for development. Many of the basic training needs are the same across the company (e.g., communications, technical skills). Of course, there will be specific needs for each person, but there are some common training needs by several employees. If someone does the research and makes it available to everyone, it saves time and frustration for the other employees. Also, company discounts can be negotiated with training providers that give the company more savings. The resource guide should provide information on how to get those discounts. Keep in mind that a Training Resource Guide can be a simple document or online resource that grows as more training resources are found.

While the company should provide the structure and a budget for talent development, it is ultimately the employee's responsibility to take ownership of his or her own development.

STRENGTHS-BASED DEVELOPMENT

Managing employees by focusing and developing their strengths is called Strengths-Based Development. The basis of this approach is that people are simply better at some things than others, and that people are more fulfilled and productive when they spend more time doing the things that they are good at. Strengths-Based Development is about helping employees reach their potential by focusing on what is innately "right" with them instead of just focusing on what is "wrong."

> Everybody is a genius, but if you judge a fish by its ability to climb a tree, it will live its whole life believing it is stupid.
> — ALBERT EINSTEIN (PINOLA, 2011)

Gallup conducted an extensive study of strength-based management practices involving 1.2 million employees across 22 organizations. The study found that 90% of the companies that implemented strength-based management practices had performance increases at or above the following ranges:

- 10% to 19% increased sales
- 14% to 29% increased profit
- 3% to 7% higher customer engagement
- 6% to 16% lower turnover (low-turnover organizations)
- 26% to 72% lower turnover (high-turnover organizations)
- 9% to 15% increase in engaged employees
- 22% to 59% fewer safety incidents

Further, Gallup reports that "67% of employees who strongly agree that their manager focuses on their strengths are *engaged* in their jobs. When employees strongly disagree with this statement, the percentage of engaged workers plummets to 2%." (Cooper S. , 2016)

How do you develop this magic ingredient for engagement? First, you need to find out what strengths your employees possess. Gallup recommends using the CliftonStrengths assessment which provides in-depth information on an employee's talents. However, you could do something as simple as observing and getting to know your employees. If you look closely enough, you can generally see the innate talent.

You could also survey employees on where they think their strengths lie and what they enjoy doing. This could be part of the performance management program. You could have employees complete a self-assessment *prior* to the annual review and return it to you several days before the meeting. This gives you time to prepare development options in advance of the meeting, which makes it more efficient and effective.

Another option is to place some questions in the performance review form for the manager to discuss with the employee during the performance review. Provided below are examples of the questions you could ask in the self-assessment form or performance review form:

- What did you enjoy working on this past year? Why?

- What do you feel are your *natural* talents and abilities? How can we help you develop those to reach your full potential?

- What type of work gives you energy?

- What motivates and inspires you?

- Do you feel that your talents are being fully utilized in your job? If no, how could that be improved?

By tying the strengths assessment to the performance management program, it helps ensure that the discussion and development actually happen. It becomes part of the annual process, not something that managers need to try to fit somewhere in their schedules. Development probably won't happen if it is not part of the company's processes.

After you find the employee's natural talents, look for opportunities for him or her to use and develop those talents.

MANAGER TRAINING

The greatest leader is not necessarily the one
who does the greatest things. He is the one that
gets the people to do the greatest things.

— RONALD REAGAN (WINDUST, 2015)

In Gallup's *State of the American Workplace* study, they found that companies whose workforce is made up of at least 75% of engaged employees are doing two things right:

1.   Providing ongoing training and tools for managers to increase engagement of their people

2.   Carefully selecting managers

It is frequently stated that people leave bad bosses, not companies. According to a Gallup study, 50% of employees leave because of their bosses. So, doesn't it make sense to make manager training a priority? *Even if you have to pay to have managers trained, it would cost you less than losing employees and/ or having employees who are not engaged.*

> **50% of employees leave because of their bosses.**
> — GALLUP

To be a great manager, the person must be a great coach. Bill McCartney said, "All coaching is, is taking a player where he can't take himself." One of the most significant ways to improve engagement is to develop managers into great coaches. This is because coaching is an *ongoing* intentional process. *Can you imagine if a coach didn't work with his players between games, and then wondered why they lost?* That is preposterous, and so is not coaching employees on an ongoing basis and wondering why they did not have good performance!

Now, I'm from the great state of Alabama, so I know something about winning coaches. In fact, I worked at the Paul W. Bryant Museum in college. (Yes, the University of Alabama has a football museum.) Winning coaches can teach us a lot about managing people and teams. Here are just some of the characteristics of winning coaches from which managers can learn:

- **Recruit Top Talent**. Coach Nick Saban is known for his stellar college football recruiting process, which has gained him six national championships. One of the reasons top players from around the country play for Coach Saban is because of the large number of players who have gone on to play in the NFL. Coach Saban is known for *developing* his players to reach the next level, and that is where they get paid the big bucks! It is reported that he keeps a list of his former players who are in the NFL and their salaries. He shows this list to players he is trying to recruit.

  Managers who can tell candidates about their development process and even show the results of the program (e.g., Bob got a promotion last year, Sally got her MBA which was paid for by the company) have a better chance of winning top talent. *Do you have a development program worth promoting?* If not, build one!

- **Teambuilding**. Coach Mike Krzyzewski said, "A common mistake among those who work in sport is spending a disproportional amount of time on 'x's and o's' as compared to time spent learning about people." A great coach knows each player's strengths and weaknesses. He knows how to use the talents of each player, and then work to the strengths of each player to build a great team.

  Coach Bear Bryant said, "You must learn how to hold a team together. You must lift some men up, calm others down, until finally they've got one heartbeat. Then you've got yourself a team." (Cooper, 2012) *How effective would your team be if they were working with one heartbeat?*

  Managers need to understand each employee's strengths and weaknesses. Deploy and build on each individual's strengths; they will be happier, and the team will be stronger. Generally, where one person is weak, another is strong, so working to each individual's strengths helps overcome the weaknesses.

Coach Saban has his players take a personality test each year so he and his coaches know how to bring the best out of each player. Personality tests are a great way for managers to learn how each employee thinks and to improve his/her effectiveness.

- **Develop the Whole Person**. Great coaches constantly develop the skills of their players and help ensure that they are in good shape *physically* and *mentally*. Coaches care about the health of their players because they know that they can't perform well if they are not healthy. The same is true for employees.

  Some managers focus only on the goal and do not think about how they are tearing down their greatest asset – their people. If employees are working so many hours that they do not have time to exercise, eat healthy (instead of grabbing fast food), and get enough sleep, they will not be as effective and will probably leave.

  > Some managers focus only on the goal and do not think about how they are tearing down their greatest asset – their people.

  Also, vacation time is important for an employee to get refreshed and spend time with friends and family. Employees should not be treated with resentment when they take earned time off. Nor should they be on call or do work during vacation. Running employees into the ground eventually leads to a loss of productivity and probably the employees themselves, and they are not easily replaced.

While there are a lot of winning coaches, there are also a lot of coaches who consistently have losing records. Frequently, these coaches are dismissed. They may have been great players, but they are not cut out for coaching.

In the same way, not everyone is designed to be a manager. If someone is trained and coached, but just does not have the ability or willingness to manage people, *they should not be in that position*. It will cause employees to leave. I suggest moving the supervisor to a non-supervisory role. If that is not possible, you may need to let him/her go and replace him/her with someone who does have good management skills.

CHAPTER 23

Total Rewards Communication

COMMUNICATIONS IS WHAT BRINGS THE Total Rewards strategy to life. It won't do you any good to have the best Total Rewards package if you don't communicate it to your employees. If an employee does not know and value all that you are providing him (financial and non-financial), how can he or she appreciate it? If the employees don't appreciate it, you are losing money and probably employees.

People who understand and value their entire employment package are more likely to stay with that company. If another company tries to lure them away with a shiny object (e.g., higher salary, promotion), they are better educated to ask about the *entire* employment package. Employees with a Total Rewards mindset can see past the shiny object and require more from another company before taking the leap.

HOW TO CREATE A TOTAL REWARDS MINDSET

Implementing a Total Rewards program is moving from being tactical (short-term focus on individual programs) to strategic (long-term focus on the entire employment deal). Therefore, Total Rewards communications should also be a strategic long-term plan. This communication plan should build understanding and commitment, and influence behavioral change over time. Taking a strategic, long-term communication and education approach and moving employees from a passive mindset to an engaged, committed perspective is an integral part of the Total Rewards communication process.

After you have created your Total Rewards strategy, there are some key communication programs that you need to establish right away.

1. Launch to Existing Employees

The Total Rewards launch should create excitement about the company's new strategic focus on enhancing employee programs and the work environment. It should say to the employees that what is important to them is important to the company. The launch should include learning more about what employees want and need – developing an ongoing dialogue.

In the Total Rewards launch, you should give an overview of all of the employee programs offered to them (refer to the Total Rewards inventory list). Bring everything together to help them see the programs as a whole, which is more valuable than individual programs. If you are adding a new program(s), this should be included as well.

The Total Rewards launch should communicate that the company is focused on ensuring employees receive the most from their employment programs. To emphasize this, have a few education programs lined up that you can announce (e.g., a healthcare provider teaching about how to use their wellness program).

Tell them about any new plans for understanding their needs better (e.g., focus group, survey). The launch meeting is also a great time to ask employees for feedback on areas that they would like to receive more education and training.

When we launched Total Rewards at Scandipharm, we had a luncheon for employees and gave a presentation on the new strategy. We also had promotional items from some benefit providers that we gave away. People love free stuff – no matter how small! For employees in the sales force, we gave a webinar presentation and provided in-person education on programs at sales meetings.

The Total Rewards launch can be fancy with a new logo, t-shirts, or whatever fits your culture. It can also be very simple without a lot of fuss. The important thing is that you communicate!

2. Integrate into the Recruiting Process

Create recruiting tools aligned with your Total Rewards message. You want people to see the value of your employment deal and know that the company takes a strategic approach to managing those programs. Since people are attracted by the whole work experience, you want applicants to see the importance that the company places on non-financial as well as financial rewards. You want applicants to see that you get it! They are a whole person interested in more than just compensation and benefits.

This is another area where digging for the gold in your current programs pays off. Many employers simply don't think to promote things, such as a free wellness program offered by their healthcare provider, as a benefit. Since you've gone through the exercise of creating your Total Rewards strategy, you have a more comprehensive program to promote. Also, in creating your strategy, you identify what makes your company unique, which helps in setting you apart from your competitors trying to lure the same top talent.

To get the Total Rewards message out to applicants, work with your recruiters to enhance their current communications to job applicants. Also, provide them with the Total Rewards inventory list to use as a "cheat sheet" when discussing with employees.

3. Onboarding Process

Continue the Total Rewards message in the onboarding process. I recommend presenting new hire employment papers in a nice pocket folder with the words 'Total Rewards' on the front. Instead of handing a new employee a stack of papers to sign and documents to read, the Total Rewards folder further enforces the value that the company places on its programs.

The pocket folder could be as simple as a plain folder with a printed label on the front, or you could have nice folders printed. Either way, it doesn't have to cost a lot of money to increase the perceived value of your programs and start employees off with a positive view of their employment package.

ONGOING COMMUNICATIONS

After the person has been sold on the company and gone through the onboarding process, they still need to be continuously sold on the company. Even after you've recruited an employee, other recruiters will still try to steal them away from you. While technology has made the recruiting process better, it also keeps the doors open to thieves. Surround your castle with good communications. Fewer of your employees will be stolen by bandits.

The relationship with employees is like any other relationship. You have to keep investing time and effort to keep it alive. Employees need to be constantly reminded of the programs that the company offers them and why it is a great place to work. This takes some effort, but not as much effort as recruiting and training a new employee. Think of it as preventive medicine.

Provided below are some ways to create ongoing communications.

1. Lunch and Learn

Hold lunch and learn meetings to educate employees on different portions of your Total Rewards package. These meetings can be provided by someone from your company or outside benefit providers. For example, you could invite your 401(k) provider to talk about your plan, and he might even provide the lunch.

Also, ask benefit providers for some of their free promotional items to give to your employees. People generally love these giveaways, and it promotes your company's program. One time, a healthcare provider gave our employees blue stress balls, and those balls were thrown around the office for years, frequently at an unsuspecting employee! It was all in good fun and broke up the day with some laughter.

If there is an area that people just do not seem to understand or have a lot of questions about, a lunch and learn will help with this problem. Stock-based compensation (stock options, ESPP, restricted share units, etc.) was my niche area at Scandipharm. I provided a lot of training on this topic because people (even executives) have difficulty understanding these complex programs. Stock-based compensation is designed to motivate employees to act as stock holders and drive up the price of the stock. Also, they are designed to be "golden handcuffs" that motivate people to stay with the company. If an employee doesn't understand the potential value of the award and how he or she can improve the value, the stock-based compensation isn't serving its purpose. Effective communications are critical to achieving success with more complex programs.

2. Total Rewards Statements
Total Rewards statements are an annual report on how much the employer spent on the employee during the year. It includes *everything* that an employer spends, including taxes, bonuses, cost of benefits, workers compensation, 401(k) contributions, awards, training, etc. When the costs are added up, it is staggering and gives the employee a different picture of how much their employment deal with the company is worth. Employees simply don't think about all that the employer is paying on their behalf. The Total Rewards statements are a mindset shifter, even for those of us who work in HR.

The reward statements are designed for engagement and retention. The employee feels more valued when they see the large amount of money that the employer pays for them to work there. Additionally, it gives employees a greater reason to turn away other suiters.

There are many companies that will create Total Rewards statements for you. I suggest that you shop around to find the best fit for you. The company will provide you with the design for the statement, and you will provide the data.

3. Align with Processes

Enhance communications around processes such as performance management, benefit enrollment, and compensation. Use these touchpoints to remind employees of the Total Rewards package. When doing training or giving a presentation on any program, I always start with a slide, showing the whole Total Rewards package. Then I say that we are focusing on a certain segment of that package (e.g., compensation) today. Always, bring people back to the Total Rewards picture to remind them of the whole.

Elements of the Total Rewards program

Finally, I want to leave you with a few more tips on communication.

- Utilize a variety of communication vehicles (e.g., email, posters, webinars, in-person presentations). Remember, people learn in different ways. It generally takes hearing something three times to remember it.

- Make it easy for your employees to access information on the programs that you offer. If you have an employee portal, make information on your employee programs easily accessible on the portal.

- Your communications will be stronger if you get support from the managers.

Communication is vital to the success of your Total Rewards program. Strategic communications improve your return on investment in employee programs. Additionally, communications improve your ability to attract, engage, and retain high-caliber employees, which ultimately leads to achieving Magnetic Advantage.

CONCLUSION

I'VE GIVEN YOU A LOT of ideas, resources, and strategies to create Magnetic Advantage in your company. Now it is up to you to choose what will work for you. You and your company are unique, so find that perfect mix that will give you the edge in recruiting top talent, retaining them and keeping them engaged.

Finally, I want to leave you with some Zig Ziglar encouragement.

- *Success is not a destination; it is a journey.*

- *You already have every characteristic necessary for success if you recognize, claim, develop, and use them.*

- *Man is designed for accomplishment, engineered for success, and endowed with the seeds of greatness.*

- *Failure is an event. Not a person.*

- *Don't be distracted by criticism. Remember – the only taste of success some people have is when they take a bite out of you.*

- *If you don't like who you are and where you are, don't worry about it because you're not stuck either with who you are or where you are. You can grow. You can change. You can be more than you are.*

- *What you get by achieving your goals is not nearly as important as what you become by achieving your goals.*

I am honored to carry on the legacy of Zig Ziglar. I hope that this book will be a blessing to you and help you to become the winner that you were born to be!

BIOGRAPHY

PASCHA KELLEY is a Ziglar Legacy Certified trainer with twenty years of human resources experience. The majority of her corporate work experience was with a start-up pharmaceutical company that grew to a global multi-million-dollar organization. Through this experience, Pascha has worked at many different stages of company development, and has been part of several mergers and acquisitions. She designed and implemented a broad range of employee programs to meet the needs of the ever-changing company and workforce.

As a Ziglar Legacy Certified trainer, Pascha has combined her corporate knowledge with the time-tested success principles of Zig Ziglar. She has a passion for helping people succeed in their personal and professional lives. She is a speaker, trainer, author, and consultant.

Pascha lives in Birmingham, Alabama, with her husband Mike. They have a blended family with six kids: Cori, Stephen, Kristin, Madeline, Jacob, and Sean.

BIBLIOGRAPHY

Bulygo, Z. (2013, February). Tony Hsieh, Zappos, and the Art of Great Company Culture. *KISSmetrics.com*.

Collins, J. I. (1994). *Built to Last: Successful Habits of Visionary Companies*. New York, NY: HarperCollins Publishers, Inc.

Cooper, J. (2012). Top 50 Quotes from Bear Bryant. *saturdaydownsouth.com*.

Cooper, S. (2016, October 24). Why Aren't All Organizations Strength-Based? *gallup.com*.

Drysdale, C. (2017). 8 Brilliant Quotes from Workplace Culture Innovators. *octanner.com*.

Elton, A. G. (2007, 2009). *The Carrot Principle*. New York: Free Press.

Franklin, B. (2011). *The Way to Wealth: Ben Franklin on Money and Success*. CreateSpace Independent Publishing Platform.

Groth, A. (2012, July 24). You're the Average of the Five People You Spend the Most Time With. *businessinsider.com*.

Hakobyan, M. (2016, December 21). Are You Treating Your Employees Like People or Proccesses. *huffingtonpost.com*.

Harter, E. O. (2017, April 18). 37 Workplaces that Stand Out from the Rest. *Gallup.com*.

Hesselbein, F. (Spring 1999). The Key to Cultural Transformation. *Leader to Leader*.

Hyken, S. (2015, December 5). Drucker said 'Culture Eats Strategy for Breakfast' and Enterprise Rent-A-Car Proves It. *Forbes.com*.

Johnson, J. (2016, January 26). Employee Recognition 2016. *devinegroup.com*.

Keteyian, A. (2014, September 14). Alabama Coach Nich Saban's Quest for Perfection. *cbsnews.com*.

Maxwell, J. (1998 and 2007). *The 21 Irreputable Laws of Leadership*. Nashville, TN: Thomas Nelson.

Maxwell, J. (2007). *The 21 Indispensable Qualities of a Leader: Becoming the Person Others Will Want to Follow*. Thomas Nelson, Inc.

Pinola, M. (2011, August 16). Everyone Is a Genius. *likehacker.com*.

Ramsey, D. (2011). *EntreLeadership: 20 Years of Practical Business Wisdom for the Trenches*. Howard Books.

Roberts, R. (2015, September 16). 5 Strategies for GEE (Great Employee Engagement) by Sir Richard Branson. *enrich-hr.co.uk*.

Roskvist, K. (2017). Coaching Quotes from the Best Sports Coaches. *athleteassessments.com*.

Sears, L. (2017). *2017 Retention Report: Trends, Reasons & Recommendations*. Work Institute.

Turner, D. A. (2015). *It's My Pleasure*. Elevate Publishing, Boise, ID.

Ty West. (2016, May 31). Birmingham's Best Places to Work for 2016. *Birmingham Business Journal*, 1.

Welch, J. (2005). *Winning*. New York: Harper Business.

Windust, J. (2015, January 26). Top 76 quotes on Performance Management. *cognology.com*.

Wright, C. (2017). *Business Boutique: A Women's Guide for Making Money Doing What She Loves*. Brentwood, TN: Ramsey Press, The Lampo Group, LLC.

Ziglar, Z. (1990). *Zig Ziglar's Little Book of Big Quotes*.

Ziglar, Z. (2009). *See You at the Top: Twenty-Fifth Anniversary Edition*. Gretna: Pelican Publishing Company.

Ziglar, Z. Z. (2012). *Born to Win*. Success Books.

WANT MORE RESOURCES
TO BUILD YOUR
MAGNETIC ADVANTAGE?

Check out my website
paschakelley.com
for templates to help put the
principles from this book into action.

9 781946 629265